THE TIMES

CROSSWORD COLLECTION

TIMES BOOK[S]

Published in 2005 by Times Books

HarperCollins*Publishers*
77-85 Fulham Palace Road
Hammersmith
London W6 8JB

www.harpercollins.co.uk
Visit the book lover's website

Reprint 2

The Times is a registered trademark of
Times Newspapers Ltd

ISBN 0-00-721300-X

British Library Cataloguing in Publication Data
A catalogue record for this book is available from the British Library.

Typeset in Great Britain by Davidson Pre-Press Graphics Ltd, Glasgow G3.

Printed and bound in Great Britain by Clays Ltd, St Ives plc.

INTRODUCTION

The second crossword in this collection, published on 14 January 1998, celebrated the centenary of the death of Lewis Carroll, who doubtlessly would have excelled as a composer of cryptic crosswords had the form been invented in his lifetime. Like many Victorians, he enjoyed finding apposite anagrams, such as Flit on, cheering angel (8,11).

Another of his ingenious challenges was to rearrange the letters of the following sentence into one word: Nor do we. Like Queen Victoria herself, he composed many acrostics – lines of verse in which the first letters spelt out words. Above all, he delighted in puns; the description of "The Hunting of the Snark" as "An Agony, in Eight Fits" puns on "fit", an archaic word for "canto".

Other forms of word puzzles were his own invention. In "Doublets", one word has to be transformed into another through a chain of words each differing from its predecessor by only one letter. Thus HEAD can become TAIL via HEAL, TEAL, TELL, TALL – can you change TEARS into SMILE in the same fashion?

Crossword 56 was also topical and thematic, since it coincided with the Mind Sports Olympiad, referring to many of the games included in that event. Indeed, bridge and chess, in particular, feature directly or indirectly in many of our clues.

Further, to solve one of the clues in Crossword 30, you need to be aware that it appeared on 30 April.

I'm writing from California where I recently returned to full-time academic life, at San Diego State University. In this career, I also find Lewis Carroll had remarkable insights to offer, in particular into the nature of language in relation to mathematics.

The crosswords in the book appeared in *The Times* in 1998 and 2000.

Brian Greer
Crossword Editor of *The Times*, 1995–2000

(Answers: Florence Nightingale, one word, TEARS, SEARS, STARS, STARE, STALE, STILE, SMILE (for example)).

A BEGINNER'S GUIDE TO *THE TIMES* CROSSWORD

ACROSS

1 High-flier ruined by exposure in Sun (6)
5 Nonconformist churchman's back I protected from rain (8)
9 Opposition is hesitant to reform (10)
10 Arranger selecting odd pieces for composer (4)
11 Frosty spell in unfriendly game (4,4)
12 Characteristic tone in old instrument cut short (6)
13 Charge for conversion as gas is offered, initially (4)
15 Call artist a venomous creature (8)
18 Strange sort of small house? Indeed, it was (8)
19 Absence of authorisation for retreat (4)
21 Was mistress under stress? Sounds like it (6)
23 Specify drink – same again? (8)
25 Architect leaves sewer after fall (4)
26 Like a resistance force made up without ringleader (10)
27 American statesman noted for his Canterbury relation (8)
28 For example, miss a run (6)

DOWN

2 Censor accepts new section in poem (5)
3 They make up shower curtains artist at home put up (9)
4 "A man" finally solved her cryptic puzzle (6)
5 Maiden is under arrest? Just the opposite – that's an error (15)
6 One making late appearance (it's in a TV broadcast) (8)
7 Raise millions to modernise the forces (5)
8 Singer, no pro, gets lot wrong (9)
14 One sort of bird – and another right outside (9)
16 Leaves without the slightest difficulty (5,4)
17 Small meal? It's hard to say (8)
20 Fine Italian instruments you love in Rome (6)
22 Involved in begging, a minor? (5)
24 One in exaltation turned up round a village (5)

NOTES

ACROSS

1 ICARUS The whole clue is a cryptic definition, and has nothing to do with a tabloid scandal about a successful person. Icarus and his father Daedalus made wings to escape from Crete but Icarus flew too high and the wax securing his wings melted in the sun's rays, so he fell to his death.

5   MAVERICK = nonconformist. The rest works like an algebraic equation, thus: VER (= churchman's back) + I inside MACK (i.e. protected from rain).

9   ANTITHESIS = opposition. Anagram of IS HESITANT (indicator: to reform).

10   ARNE = composer (Thomas Arne, 1710-1778). More unusual clue type instructing solver to select odd letters (pieces) of ArRaNgEr.

11   COLD SNAP = frosty spell. Combination of COLD (= unfriendly) + SNAP (= game).

12   TIMBRE = characteristic tone. Timbrel (old instrument) is cut short.

13   AGIO = charge for conversion (when changing money). First letters (indicator: initially) of As Gas Is Offered.

15   RINGHALS = a venomous creature (large spitting cobra). Combination of RING (call) + HALS (artist).

18 FORSOOTH = indeed (note that "it was" points to the word being archaic). Anagram: SORT OF HO (ho. = small house, i.e. abbreviation) (indicator: strange).

19 NOOK = retreat. Absence of authorisation = NO OK.

21 TAUGHT = was mistress. Homophone of taut = under stress (indicator: sounds like it).

23 NAMESAKE = same again (somewhat cryptic definition signalled by question mark). Combination of NAME (specify) + SAKE (drink).

25 Two definitions. ADAM = architect/ADAM = leaves sewer after fall (Adam and Eve sewed fig-leaves to make aprons).

26 FRICTIONAL = like a resistance force. FICTIONAL (= made up) outside (without) R (= ringleader).

27 Two definitions. FRANKLIN = American statesman (Benjamin Franklin, 1706-1790/FRANKLIN = noted for his Canterbury relation. (Franklin's Tale is one of the Canterbury Tales).

28 Two definitions. SINGLE = for example, miss (i.e. an unmarried person)/SINGLE = a run.

DOWN

2 CANTO = section in poem. CATO = censor (Marcus Porcius Cato, elected censor in 184, famous for his zeal in that capacity), contains (accepts) N = new.

3 RAINDROPS = they make up shower. DROPS = curtains, with RA = artist) + IN (= at home) on top (put up).

4 The whole clue is a cryptic definition. The SPHINX was a female monster inhabiting the district around Thebes, who set the riddle "What animal walks on four legs in the morning, two at noon, and three in the evening?". Oedipus finally provided the answer "A man", who crawls as a baby, walks upright in mid-life, and with the aid of a stick in old age.

5 MISAPPREHENSION = an error. M (= maiden) + IS on top of (under? Just the opposite) APPREHENSION (= arrest).

6 VISITANT = one making late appearance (a visitant is a ghost, i.e. late = dead person). Anagram: IT'S IN A TV (indicator: broadcast).

7 REARM = modernise the forces. Combination of REAR (= raise) + M (= millions, abbreviation).

8 CONTRALTO = singer. Combination of CONTRA (= no pro) + anagram of LOT (indicator: wrong).

14 GOOSANDER = one sort of bird. AND with GOOSE (= another (bird)) + R (= right, abbreviation) outside.

16 Two definitions. HANDS DOWN = leaves (i.e. bequeaths)/HANDS DOWN = without the slightest difficulty.

17 Two definitions. MOUTHFUL = small meal/MOUTHFUL = it's hard to say.

20 Two definitions. AMATIS = fine Italian instruments (plural of Amati)/AMATIS = you love in Rome (amo, amas, amat, amamus, amatis ...)

22 The whole clue acts both as a definition (GAMIN is a street urchin who might be involved in begging) and hidden clue – begginG A MINor (indicator: involved in).

24 KRAAL = village. LARK (= one in exaltation, exaltation being the collective noun for larks) inverted (turned up), containing (round) A.

THE PUZZLES

1

ACROSS

1 Adjourned for some wine (4)
3 Academic stream is beside itself (4)
6 Add a little terse advice to convertible driver in rain? (3,2)
10 Red nose, perhaps, that Continental got in fight (7)
11 (For course) Q: Where did Charles hide after Worcester? (7)
12 Approval given by merry socialist in speech (4,5)
13 Verse of *Abide with Me*, say, cut short in divinity lesson (5)
14 Scholar took exam, securing first place (6)
16 Conductor's turn with part of the orchestra (8)
18 Shot in two parts of body (8)
19 Break in bay (6)
22 Shortly about to run off without paying for this orange (5)
23 Alert goalkeeper may dive thus (2,3,4)
25 Filled with enthusiasm, return to log support (7)
26 One holds one's breath – it may go up (7)
27 Spencer jacket ultimately distinctive in style (5)
28 Reduce intake for legislative assembly (4)
29 Labour, generally, having it in for press? (4)

DOWN

1 Dressed in frills, Elizabeth Bennet initially had cold shoulders (7)
2 Brains are needed in this case (5)
4 Appeal to deflect god (6)
5 Sudden guess that produces negative result (8)
6 Urgent bid to reconstruct city hence protest letters, reputedly (9,5)
7 Non-exclusive way to communicate official policy (5,4)
8 As payment for part of chapter, turn in advance? (7)
9 Failure to relax, as result of driving compulsion? (7,7)
15 Intelligent, omitting line in travel document? The other way round (4,5)
17 Die clutching neck filled with blood (8)
18 Gain advantage, having been out to attack (7)
20 Justice of the Peace (7)
21 Famous birthplace definitely established (6)
24 Acceptable in European city, being head-over-heels in it? (5)

ACROSS

1 Knight among more cult characters turned out a sad creature (4,6)
6 Piece of card (4)
10 He came to a dreadful end, in agony (5)
11 Any recent novel writer has one today (9)
12 Gave evidence in trial, one launched after Queen's loss (9)
13 Bill lacking in power of speech (5)
14 One turning into a pig on the way? (4,3)
15 Argued in court quietly, like old-fashioned type (7)
17 In sorry state, is lad in mess? Off with their heads! (7)
19 Thanks to *Through the Looking-Glass*, initially, Queen's seen as gossip (7)
21 Some opera's said to be very musical (5)
23 Quiet tear about farewell – not unusual (9)
24 Regularly walk and run – it shows odd behaviour (5,4)
25 Girl not reflecting and plunging into adventures (5)
26 Repeatedly act as race organiser (4)
27 Country looking fantastic visited after fall (10)

DOWN

1 Nameless horrible creature catching Boots, initially a member of the gang (7)
2 Support for a growing girl's need (4,5)
3 Girl hushed Kitty, endlessly shaken? It's sweet (7,7)
4 Shaking violently following wild creature – no end of quest (7)
5 Joined with king going in a file (5,2)
7 I run with a queen, one inhabitant of divided land? (5)
8 County Nell and Edward reached at last (7)
9 Powerlessly falling in earth, I have a peculiar resistance (7-4-3)
16 A really good time to produce TV broadcast with 25 (5,4)
17 Hit suddenly distributes cards, going up about two metres (7)
18 Noted female, thoroughly wet, had a race – with duck (7)
19 Laughed to observe next tea being announced (3,4)
20 Take steps again to enjoy book afresh – about time (7)
22 Queen gave off about such a small amount of evidence? (5)

3

ACROSS

1 Conceited youngster, a future skipper, possibly (4)
3 Water very quietly absorbed in part of body (5,5)
10 Promotion of number one (4-11)
11 A barrier to progress for some races (8)
12 One watched for a shot that delights a golfer (6)
14 Wade across one? Hardly! (5)
16 Reprimand from oriental king tolerated (7-2)
18 One person's tale is inaccurate about female politician (4,5)
19 No longer taxes people up North (5)
20 Mouse taken to guy (6)
22 Fellow's agitation describing dons (8)
26 It's said to be a careless error (4,2,3,6)
27 Book individual after arrest, finding part of skeleton (10)
28 Characters in front of queue, say, in dominant position (4)

DOWN

1 The type who bothers with duck sauce (5)
2 Eliminate European side at Lord's (6,3)
4 Liberal university in commitment that distributes power (10)
5 Times supporting a chap such as Douglas? (4)
6 Drinks provided in wild parties (9)
7 Fraudulent type raised charges by minimal amount (5)
8 Seen to run off between you and me (5,4)
9 Facts making American a little upset (4)
13 Disc that's likely to be hit soon after launch (4,6)
14 The airs that people put on! (4,5)
15 Ancient intriguing led to her death (9)
17 Model of chivalry pronounced the latest word? (9)
21 Hot and sick after getting cold like this (5)
23 Sort of memory that follows piano concert (4)
24 Penny each, possibly (5)
25 Objections raised in short piece (4)

4

ACROSS

1 Contract that's set up between banks? (7)
5 One river or another – to another returned (7)
9 Stories of Italian love or of French romance, possibly (9)
10 Disc made of iron used in combat (5)
11 Friend in fur not getting chill (5)
12 Outstanding return for county's brilliant star (9)
14 Book that's good, but not first edition? (7,7)
17 Change for better infernal nuisance causing embarrassment (6,8)
21 As a rule, not many are involved in it (9)
23 It makes sense to take aim (5)
24 Could be worse off as a farm worker (5)
25 Co-partner ruined, on the other hand (3,6)
26 With method arranged, carried out ambush (7)
27 Dog appears to eat into fish (7)

DOWN

1 Reckon court must put one inside as fanatic (6)
2 Admit set is incomplete (7)
3 Restrict the flow of people's expression of anger (9)
4 One presenting picture so awful about rise of EC? (11)
5 Quarter of a pint in beer container (3)
6 Keep out of ghetto, we recommend (5)
7 As if I'm distressed about old criminals! (7)
8 Conceals the end (8)
13 Little money clear person comes up with in this (7,4)
15 Mental confusion, losing head in violent downpour (9)
16 Was no safety device put up for this cutting tool? (5,3)
18 Beautiful road a driver doesn't want to leave (7)
19 Boat for which portage is less of a problem? (7)
20 Collected maps on time, in the end (2,4)
22 A case ended prematurely in these courts (5)
25 Flat sheets of paper (3)

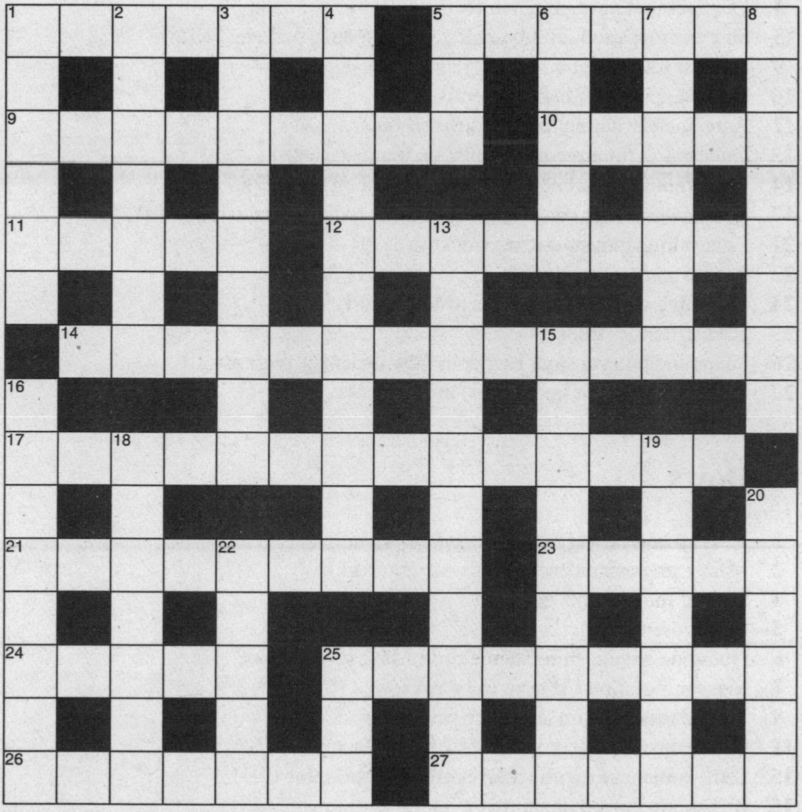
1
2
3
4
5
6
7
8
9
10
11
12
13
14
15
16
17
18
19
20
21
22
23
24
25
26
27

5

ACROSS

1 War banished from English town or one in Scotland (4)
3 Show compassion, and be able to follow suit, perhaps (4,1,5)
9 Look at some bimbo gleefully? (4)
10 House appears to shake, note (10)
12 Agreement whereby pet's restricted on rope (9)
13 Facility left for support of artistic effort (5)
14 One produces shares for consumers in joint operation (7,5)
18 It indicates a reference showing how to make a pair of stilettos? (6,6)
21 Controlling current cricket sides (2-3)
22 Assess performance of stroke on the river (4-5)
24 Charming company who had to leave early (10)
25 Told to deliver trunk (4)
26 I examine two cardinal points in new order for recruits (10)
27 Modern copper on beat's seen the light (4)

DOWN

1 Turn up and bowl first in the game (8)
2 Master preparing courses shows such skill (8)
4 Having more points each (5)
5 It's all there is (9)
6 Does one have a slim chance of holding up a casino? (5,2,5)
7 Make suggestion I'd save to be reviewed (6)
8 Turned this creature the other way up (6)
11 Disastrous sequence of events, after a knock-on? (6,6)
15 Start to risk cash with small northern negotiator (2-7)
16 British governor general (8)
17 Suddenly stop riding? Time to get your skates on! (6-2)
19 Hunting call making the majority of you sick, possibly (6)
20 Do I find a good deal useful as a club member? (6)
23 Sort out the problem of crack (5)

ACROSS

1 Run in a straight line (6)
4 Continental community still over the moon (8)
10 Fat cat apt to curl in a strange way (9)
11 Some meat enjoyed like this? (5)
12 Leftover old insecticide overcomes people (7)
13 Followers always holding one back (7)
14 Try something desperate – as greedy suckers do? (6,2,6)
19 Sexy beauty with part to play in historical record (6,8)
21 Having completed short time in firm (7)
24 Catch unknown creature – a parrot (7)
26 Liquor is found inside part of supermarket (5)
27 In bad-tempered case, I am willing to appear as witness (9)
28 Choke – one of car's controls (8)
29 Soldier discovering fish by a river (6)

DOWN

1 Heartlessly pay dole in new way – spread out (6)
2 Song sequence about love put off (9)
3 Clubs get beaten in the end (5)
5 React violently to pander (5)
6 Country's temperature the man reports (3,6)
7 Bird – an enormous creature (5)
8 Talk? Just the opposite (8)
9 Fancy needlework covering tail of shirt (8)
15 Aggressive exchange you reported fast (9)
16 Actors of limited range may be of two sorts (8)
17 Wicked actor somehow promises to settle scores (9)
18 Steal Jack's territory (8)
20 The old leading man comes around – he shows persistence (6)
22 One gets up part of flight (5)
23 Enable old husband to get put up in accommodation (5)
25 Soldier, without fuel, sent North on horse (5)

ACROSS

1   Plan to have no end of peace in this cathedral (8)
6   A lefty's revolutionary allegiance (6)
9   Supported rail and put in a line, in transport deal (10)
10   Star reflected in river (4)
11   Delightful person who entertains angelic bunch (8,4)
13   One captured by Spain, calamitously (4)
14   Where missile is pointed (4-4)
17   Way in which infantrymen strike gently, then hard (8)
18   Spread a little butter to end of slice (4)
20   Chap's chortling – it's killing (12)
23   Trollope's Irish member and another European (4)
24   Manager introduces band with top-class amplifier? (7,3)
25   Cage bird initially popular (6)
26   Worry and hang about, showing sign of anxiety (8)

DOWN

2   Old banger costing little that doesn't start (4)
3   Hooligan, thrown out, goes up the wall (9)
4   Tree rodent seen on bark (6)
5   Unreliable person – not to be found lurking in Ireland? (5,2,3,5)
6   Extremely poor payment poet's fortunate to get (8)
7   Embarrass, joining a party (5)
8   One's part in compilation of ten centuries? (10)
12   Being shot away? (2,8)
15   Protective cover for book (9)
16   Revolutionary acquires aristocratic title in the long run (8)
19   Blow in the band (6)
21   As Anglican, depressed by man's nature (5)
22   Sign a top rugby player (4)

8

ACROSS

1 Expert injecting horse in pain (4)
3 Schoolmaster's not hard-hearted as employer (4)
6 Father has to admit giving a dirty look (5)
10 Large animal in stream in Indian territory (7)
11 Way round hostile defensive bulge (7)
12 Topping loaf consumed by creature (9)
13 Ring route repaired (5)
14 I, for one, may be heard making this affirmation (6)
16 Victoria, for example, having time at home with Albert (8)
18 He rooted for reform, being a Roosevelt (8)
19 Drop into court in recess (6)
22 Callas, say, making mark with operatic performance (5)
23 Many an Anglo-Saxon runner initially needed a drink (9)
25 The first fruit peeled, we hear, at St. Clement's (7)
26 List that's including Times, possibly (7)
27 Person taking shot is less forward (5)
28 Go down to find place where vessels get washed up (4)
29 Dishonest grass (4)

DOWN

1 School subject a learner, for example, gets up with support (7)
2 Spartan king in a muddle (5)
4 Constant interference (6)
5 Surrendered, game being up without warning (8)
6 Shadow M? It's just a game (6-2-6)
7 Subtle implications arising from Nero's vote (9)
8 Illegitimate type of selection (7)
9 Hide with Dirk – it's to do with espionage (5-3-6)
15 Such dishes get a warm reception (4-5)
17 Buildings in the grounds (8)
18 Rough girls damaging my boots (7)
20 Only just touching a chap with sunburn (7)
21 Flag-officer? (6)
24 Stomach something ridiculous (5)

9

ACROSS

1 Tribute one in PR agency organised (9)
6 Plant that is cut by doctor died (5)
9 One hoarding two grand in back tax (7)
10 Consider a description of what happened (7)
11 Eccentric with old hat seen about (5)
12 One who arranges or, alternatively, a singer (9)
13 Live English concerts initially associated with Henry Wood (5)
14 Problem choppers might have fixing old, old hatchet (9)
17 Withdraws claws (9)
18 Best? Yes and no (5)
19 A nasty striver – one pushing in? (9)
22 This is a likely source for fibre (5)
24 Novel from Virginia or a place in Florida (7)
25 Woman being contrary about awfully good witticism (7)
26 Girl of three months, the first (5)
27 Is allowed to pick this blossom? (9)

DOWN

1 Horse pulled beer round (5)
2 Late shifts, perhaps (9)
3 Ammunition found in rubbish heaps going off (9)
4 Having had the wind up, manage to survive (4,3,3,5)
5 Operation in theatre, in new surroundings (6,2,7)
6 Yank's jailed coming from Peru, once (5)
7 Objections about love matches (5)
8 Pour cold water on fellow cleaner (9)
13 Steps taken to manage a star (5,4)
15 Turtle will bask here at first when at sea (9)
16 Opener in county's team (9)
20 Sovereign measure (5)
21 Old-fashioned record producer (5)
23 Less convincing work by Debussy (5)

10

ACROSS

1   Green's the shade for this rock (9)
6   Appear unexpectedly to be pawn ahead (3,2)
9   Bird getting stronger, gaining weight (7)
10 Account for Times appearing in English flat (7)
11 Is it odd of me to join this game? (5)
12 Lacking a match, with no pair, we hear, in love (9)
13 What makes a powerful body, or a heavenly one (8)
15 Given money to eat (4)
19 The French backs have a name for it? (4)
20 Provide care in short time, nurse having lost her head (8)
23 Advertisement about time for showing up poor linesman (9)
24 Sort of fund liable to melt away? (5)
26 Start to lose one's temper (4,3)
27 From which potential soldiers shoot (7)
28 Wine initially tasting satisfactory (5)
29 Clear, using special axe on tree (9)

DOWN

1   Relatively unimportant action the army is in, but not RAF (5,4)
2   A precept for Gorky, say (5)
3   Dashing spray hid the location of launches (8)
4   Material for dress – and there's no end of wild parties coming round (8)
5   Cast off, following this direction (6)
6   Common lacks centrepiece – a tree (6)
7   Position fitting beneficiaries of patronage exactly! (9)
8   Piece of glass left in section of door (5)
14 Distinctive sign to invest in sterling, perhaps? (9)
16 One's not fancied getting run in black stockings (4,5)
17 Harte put in agonised toil to create book (8)
18 Room for fighter with arrogance to step out (8)
21 Flier eating chop and banger (6)
22 Have trouble breathing? Fine, take steps to get round it (6)
23 Guide one into story (5)
25 Uncompromising politician shows some deceitful traits (5)

11

ACROSS

1 Surreptitious way to get Cockney well (8)
5 Colonialist that used to have colossal statue (6)
9 Warning: name to be used as spelled for legal purposes (8)
10 Secret animal in this labyrinth? Just the opposite (6)
12 Unaided battle to secure plant (8,4)
15 Decisively defeats opposition party on thc right (5)
16 Treasury stars he's brought in (9)
18 Nothing needed at table except this bread? (9)
19 Store has incomplete seal (5)
20 Imposed diet or non-civil assembly (5,7)
24 Modest cover is revived? (6)
25 Brought back to conscious state (8)
26 Very quick delivery arriving on foot, perhaps (6)
27 Taking pledge – eighteen, of course? (8)

DOWN

1 Like this, paper is easy to cut (4)
2 Noble organ loft frequently abandoned (4)
3 Sole, tuna, and tail of whiting cooked as seafood (9)
4 Repeat prescription that covers pet (4,2,3,3)
6 Sun god's burden – must banish cold (5)
7 Child denied treat might produce desired answer (2,3,5)
8 Celebrated girls given light protection (10)
11 Spectacular way to learn history, in two senses (3,2,7)
13 One spotted next to green room, daydreaming (5,5)
14 Like dismissed monk, not working (3,2,5)
17 Die in a limited rising (9)
21 Put these people on drug? That's the idea (5)
22 Part of ship made of very immature oak? (4)
23 PM once announced such a lot of changes (4)

12

ACROSS

1 Herb a little woman found in the grass (8)
6 Almost provide complete contents for short book of pictures (6)
9 Former king suffering setback at Salamis, initially (6)
10 Many high-flyers get into this other type of crossword – and put a spurt on (5,3)
11 One trying to stop fighting of turbulent marrieds (8)
12 New missile contract (6)
13 Noise of engine, entering Victoria turned low (5)
14 Block that's part of prison? Not according to Lovelace (9)
17 It's terrible to evict drunk, but that's an order (9)
19 Modest grade got by girl in form (5)
22 Writer departs with a letter for Corinthians (6)
23 Is this clock incapable of striking one? (8)
24 Fare from India – fellow returned it with thanks (8)
25 Indication of constant pressure is nothing to lawyers (6)
26 A tint I developed for red hair (6)
27 Mean American smashed advertisement about Western (8)

DOWN

2 Place of work the French set up that's used in art, especially (7)
3 Times going into project with a stance put together (9)
4 Pick up a summary (6)
5 It may result in time being ten to two, say (8,7)
6 Iron skirt and edges of negligee suitable for woman (8)
7 Turned up stuff on whale in island (7)
8 Sheep shelters found round South-West, over the hill here? (9)
13 One food store caught in check, in other words (9)
15 Protest by workers about Jack's informal contact with public (9)
16 Produce order, say, to impose restrictions (8)
18 Man appearing ragged in torn piece of cloth (7)
20 Composer of some crosswords met an aficionado (7)
21 New shoot appears about then (6)

13

ACROSS

1 Character with whom it's rash to play poker, for a start (4-5)
6 Jazz work broadcaster half-heartedly introduced (5)
9 A herb gardener's first planted in row (5)
10 Kowtowing to get honour, in case that's corrupt (9)
11 Reserve gets point, going on pitch (7)
12 Oval ball rebounds in various directions (7)
13 Finally, a certain envelope for me by way of bonus (3,4,7)
17 Extremely restrained, but it covered a great deal of ground (14)
21 Unkempt hair finally taken off (7)
23 Child teacher abandoned in capital, a wicked city (7)
25 Excess population proves disastrously harmful (9)
26 Party-goer in right state (5)
27 Rejected dictionary word suggesting alternative for 28, say (5)
28 Punch, for example, meets with tolerance in rough-and-tumble (9)

DOWN

1 Elegant clothing provided to order (8)
2 One put on the floor by such a tackle? (5)
3 Deserve to muddle one labouring in the dock (9)
4 Excited by a function held by staff (7)
5 Arrive earlier, parking on slope backwards (7)
6 Grab a silver piece for boy (5)
7 Second-best individual accepting a role as emperor (9)
8 Old policeman useful in the kitchen (6)
14 One taking part in fight with the monarch's side? (9)
15 Poet endlessly interrupting the blighter, another poet (9)
16 Fish thrashing about – it's angry (8)
18 A worm, husband behaving despicably (7)
19 Most of Taurus included in local type of star cluster (7)
20 Middling warm? Severe heat (6)
22 Girl with love that could make cowboy a good catch? (5)
24 Take aim in uniform (5)

14

ACROSS

1 Some of a brick structure (6)
5 A beautiful creature about to supply drink (8)
10 Turned mushrooms into a more-or-less risky investment (4)
11 Stay calm and endure punishment, Midshipman (4,2,4)
12 Gun's part is to blast gap in fortifications, we hear (6)
13 Beauty treatment's price due to be altered (8)
14 Contribute to act (4,1,4)
18 Chinese philosophical principle used in, for example, contemplation (5)
19 Authorised to go with expedition (5)
20 Prudence given help in training (9)
24 Recurrent suspicion about blooming programme (8)
25 One wantonly damaging museum finally left (6)
26 Colin acted badly in Western (10)
27 Daughter put in son's form (4)
28 Female turned and spoke haltingly (8)
29 Tax put on author's literary output (6)

DOWN

2 In dismay, note what goes on (7)
3 Boisterous and batty? (7)
4 In dressing, you have to draw level (7)
6 Front person – the one ruling now (9)
7 Inordinately raise rent and legal fees (9)
8 Running down upstart caught in traffic (9)
9 Fighter making escape with boat (9)
14 European right to finish quickly (6,3)
15 Like Disraeli's side, shifting allegiance endlessly (9)
16 A way to put on too much rouge going from side to side (9)
17 Wealth can supply a barrier to contain infection (9)
21 Cover up card player having accepted Bulgarian cash (7)
22 Base in which I belong has moved (7)
23 Squirrel more strenuous when love is involved (7)

15

ACROSS

1 Beat using stick (5)
4 Low accommodation, in a fashion, with little room (9)
9 This Johnny could show more éclat (9)
10 Quartz found in a mountain pass (5)
11 Movable feasts for elderly waiters (5,2,6)
14 August follower of Irish clan (4)
15 Belonging to second joint on leg, for example (10)
18 Cook's fat, and getting more dumpy (10)
19 Drug addict's employer (4)
21 Jumbo set aside – it's viciously difficult! (5,8)
24 Drop a theatrical piece (5)
25 School places for those needing remedial treatment (9)
27 Title for Sophia – one making her cross? (9)
28 Become dejected listening to Olive, say (5)

DOWN

1 Start out to look quickly inside ancient manuscript (10)
2 Settled a way round (3)
3 Cut out drill without hesitation (6)
4 Revolutionary organisation has business manager initially put in prison (9)
5 Stagger from place where one may be left in trouble (5)
6 Broadcasts are a must for those wanting play purely for enjoyment (8)
7 Insensitivity shown when one is put out (11)
8 In Baltimore we root for the pitcher (4)
12 Fitting pocket (11)
13 Presumably it can throw light on the other side (6,4)
16 Push particular goods – they help to raise sales, we hear (9)
17 Male worker concealing name still (8)
20 Thwarted, being in a place without parking (6)
22 To succeed, English knight has to go to law (5)
23 In the sound, notices a cutter (4)
26 Scene of carnival and endless wild revelry (3)

ACROSS

1 Rodent's limb cat is about to grab (6)
5 Mob's shifting alliance (8)
9 Divided up Japanese fencing, available in natural wood colour (6,4)
10 Ride gives feeling of elation (4)
11 Thought about a second one before beginning to drink (8)
12 Final instruction for beauty's toilette once? Exactly (4,2)
13 One pound rejected in country using francs (4)
15 Gun broken, relished using bare hands (8)
18 Solemn pronouncement in betting record that could pull punters in (4-4)
19 Duke making heartless premier (4)
21 Indirect route – the way one gets into security zone? (6)
23 For project, display too many pictures? (8)
25 It stops money being offered as bribe (4)
26 The first thing to stick in anyone's throat (5,5)
27 One way and another, holding a level (8)
28 Acting head, say, going into 4's payment (6)

DOWN

2 A colour nearly used for suit (5)
3 It's expedient to create simple dress (9)
4 One's housed junior officer deprived of place in France (6)
5 Ideal place for castles in the air? (5-6-4)
6 Failure to employ lower-class pundit (3-5)
7 I reduced misery round house (5)
8 Scraps with abandoned maidens, perhaps (9)
14 She takes a lot of trouble to compose her features (5,4)
16 Where one drives to get such clothes, perhaps (3,3,3)
17 African country was to ban dancing (8)
20 One detects old magistrate's sound (6)
22 Element offering new support for old craft (5)
24 Fibre finally eaten only when cooked (5)

17

ACROSS

1 Potato salad in US? As a rule, it's depressing (7,3)
6 Boss outstanding in game of cards (4)
9 In successive notes, loving to be disparaging (10)
10 Excessive concern some of us showed (4)
12 What's expert done? (12)
15 Cause of epidemic usually cut by two-thirds (9)
17 Private's less than perfect shot (5)
18 Splendid opening of tattoo in Edinburgh, okay? (5)
19 Tourists may be shown this mistake (9)
20 Where all the world was a stage? (5,7)
24 Group of students long affected by cut (4)
25 African hell-hole home to a Scot (10)
26 Pirate shot (4)
27 Meal partly cooked with sauce (10)

DOWN

1 Moderate coverage for members in part of France (4)
2 Approximate noise of bird (4)
3 Region of England in business releases (4,8)
4 Fight round roadblock, initially (3-2)
5 Fantastic rope, in a way, that can get one off the ground (9)
7 Risky thing to do in swimming race, at the end? (5-3-2)
8 Wants ideas rated differently (10)
11 Numbers of Romans to overhaul administrative organisation (5,7)
13 Rope highly tangled – it's hard to unravel (10)
14 A heartless lie to trouble enthusiast (10)
16 The sort of craze that's never longlasting? (9)
21 Perplexed, but not high and dry (2,3)
22 Substance it's right to extract from corn before grinding (4)
23 Possible conclusions reached by trial jury could be just (4)

ACROSS

1 Making no progress in set problem (6)
5 Daub page in a couple of seconds (8)
9 County's season not a productive period (8)
10 Despicable type conclusively no great shakes? (6)
11 Decorate wings of priory, bringing back more appropriate interior (8)
12 Sort of tennis the Spanish watch (8)
13 Very small measure of coffee or large 'un, perhaps (7)
16 Belgian flying from part of India (7)
20 Endlessly hang about after breakdown driving here in Austria (8)
22 Sweep – cricket stroke that's straightforward (5-3)
23 Intense anger uncalled for, with seconds out (6)
24 Late news swamped by distant crisis (8)
25 Home Guard the old, old soldier trains with? (8)
26 Excited socialist given roasting (3-3)

DOWN

2 Players hoping for a full house from pack, say? (6)
3 Element found in West when in short supply (8)
4 Crooked fence, perhaps (8)
5 A High Church point of view? (7)
6 Championship point wasted following disturbance (8)
7 Two sorts of wrong topping on a pancake (8)
8 Sort of football played in school match (5,5)
12 Can drug, say, become such a sweet substance? (5,5)
14 Trusted friend to change self-image (5,3)
15 It's not usually fair for this to be put up (8)
17 Scene that has none of the actors in (8)
18 Film star bound to go to the wall (5,3)
19 Queen captured in crazy attack (7)
21 Doubled up laughing about new Conservative leader (6)

19

ACROSS

1   Barrier that doesn't affect one's prospects (2-2)
3   Perversely blame a skit apt to be taken the wrong way (10)
9   Line of soldiers humming (4)
10 Let off dwellings where solid fuel is used (10)
12 Strait-laced girl breaking into old-fashioned language (9)
13 Fancy linc in pattcrn (5)
14 Vehicle seldom free of rattle (12)
18 Athlete keeping intellectual woman (12)
21 Coarse woman including new unconventional words (5)
22 Experience again happiness going round old city (9)
24 Feeling mere pathos, perhaps (10)
25 Car burning at centre of motorway (4)
26 Where a woman can sit after getting up (4-6)
27 Well protected, with artillery backing (4)

DOWN

1   Dance involving sailors, one form of exercise (8)
2   Not paid when old and grey, and not included (8)
4   One bowling is carrying the side – a famous spinner (5)
5   Sort of warfare soldier, say, found vigorous (9)
6   Colourful reflections produced by round trip by tube (12)
7   Vessel fatal to punters? (6)
8   Without effort, very probably (6)
11 Wordy historians? (12)
15 Discovered how circuit might be dangerous? (9)
16 Reducing strength of old unit, I become disorderly (8)
17 Correspondence about getting on outside (8)
19 Utter halfwit is kept outside tests (6)
20 Preserved – as one expects to be on the M25? (6)
23 Conservative said to be sort of pink (5)

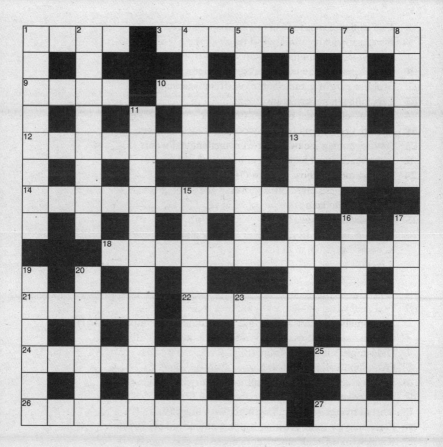

ACROSS

1 Take a chance in selection, given last word for a change (4,4)
6 Wonder if poet has finally lost money (6)
9 Marketplace accepting new sort of goat (6)
10 Relax heartless command for one who returns (8)
11 Explorer's incomplete claim rejected in island (8)
12 Revolting team's taken advantage (6)
13 Seabirds see another one returning on board (5)
14 Parasite that traditionally overlooks displays of affection (9)
17 Saw covering page by writer as something extra (9)
19 Break one's skin (5)
22 False allure of poetry prize (6)
23 One heavily criticised about nothing and taken apart (8)
24 Living off the land (8)
25 Of dusky appearance? (6)
26 Woollen material from pullover initially altered (6)
27 Rehearsal of Suite in G (8)

DOWN

2 Thoroughly examine and torture a pair of partners imprisoned (7)
3 Sea creature swallows sole, swimming in huge quantities (9)
4 Old people left inside shrine (6)
5 Overnight, I slink off, being such a shy person (9,6)
6 Doctors having gone on round found carrier of disease (8)
7 Judgment made by composer about time (7)
8 Start to recognise something hereditary in girl's size (9)
13 Party activity finds growing support around shopping centre (5,4)
15 Rivalry from Greek character accepted in good mood (9)
16 Sin that subverts real duty (8)
18 Brown is after place as tradesman (7)
20 Don, perhaps, from African country lacking capital (7)
21 Barwoman's wine, excellent when brought up (6)

ACROSS

1 Return of Verdi's opera incomplete without very great singer (4)
3 Special offer with cost finally reduced? That's natural (10)
9 Depression in the land so long (4)
10 Criminal came and left in disguise (10)
12 Washerwoman needs to use soft soap, putting in cape (9)
13 Stout is to be served inside (5)
14 Seat for parlourmaid? (7,5)
18 A pedlar, so we hear, is never taking it so easy on the road (12)
21 Mocking religious leader leaving this order (5)
22 One reckons new university projection's 100 short (9)
24 Terminate old arrangement? It depends on the strings attached (10)
25 Exempt from charge to cross river (4)
26 Evidence provided that's getting rid of monarch (10)
27 Part of cathedral, say – such as Ely? (4)

DOWN

1 Swoop down on honky-tonk with a lot of money (4-4)
2 Changing a lot, and not particularly nice about it? (8)
4 Money is stolen from a saint (5)
5 Toss up on part of square (9)
6 Way to deal with sin etc. (12)
7 Detective has to have permit for peephole (6)
8 One whose charges are small for easy task (6)
11 IOUs, possibly, for such gems? (4-8)
15 Open spaces standard for martial art (5,4)
16 Birds from the freezing poles (8)
17 A piece of armour said to inflict injury (8)
19 Blurred shot (6)
20 Finish off sauce on prawn cocktail – cover all over (6)
23 Transport system Parisians look down on? (5)

ACROSS

1 Hold in subjection in dungeon below (4,5)
6 Joins course (5)
9 Inhuman as Capek's workers were (7)
10 It's used for washing city, however backward (7)
11 Leaders in Arabia blame Yankee soldiers meddling in the Gulf (5)
12 Weather-beaten players were in tears (9)
13 Artist I encountered in Montana (5)
14 Separation of one run of three notes in advance (9)
17 Last month I got married, being weakened (9)
18 Fish that's seen between two rays (5)
19 Brave measure rejected in reform (9)
22 Visitor is supposed to speak (5)
24 Proclaim harlot's execution (7)
25 Line is a little flexible (7)
26 A number sleep before noon or practise meditation? (5)
27 Gambling activity in horse-racing centre (9)

DOWN

1 Destiny of religious leader protected by god of love (5)
2 Rudimentary mistakes by incomer (9)
3 Terms finally stated – from last month I'm linked with a corporation (9)
4 Two indict knight with corruption – and mayor (4,11)
5 Mischievous spirit or goblin of old we recollected (5,10)
6 Lily takes Abraham's nephew to the States (5)
7 In preservation, it remains of some use (5)
8 Junior officer has position and wealth (9)
13 Damaged – up to a point, 17 given treatment (9)
15 Insensitivity to pain seen from different angle in the East (9)
16 Warm spot in valley leading to old pass (9)
20 Sailor knocking out leader of the police in excitement (5)
21 Plant rising among short heather (5)
23 Lifting? It takes time to hoist (5)

23

ACROSS

1 Hence Jumbo may bring many excitement? Hard to disagree! (8)
5 Power increased by river's flow (6)
10 In which statesmen take advantage of passing the buck? (6,9)
11 More spruce getting a sprinkling of nitrate (7)
12 A city with no land set apart (7)
13 Ordered to admit composer leaving a European capital (8)
15 No use going by smell of decomposing matter (5)
18 Busy step, with a movement to the front (5)
20 Fine work of art is attractive (8)
23 Elect to enter river in the buff (7)
25 Get firm to give leave to boy (7)
26 Account I managed to turn into plenty (3-3-4-5)
27 One of Lawrence's seven wise supporters (6)
28 Old college has gone off having several unions (8)

DOWN

1 Not revealing the punishment (6)
2 Plot to immerse me in the entire Bible? (9)
3 Going for the title (7)
4 Getting on reclaimed land, dislodging the top (5)
6 Affect to have received honour? That's intolerable (3,4)
7 Animal found in East German region (5)
8 County papers clearing first page for council leader (8)
9 Such an heir father brought up – mother, too, perhaps (8)
14 King of Wessex's firm, banishing daughter without roof over head (8)
16 Maiden in Nebraska overcoming barrier to become brave's wife (9)
17 Disadvantage of useful-sounding EC policy (8)
19 Run out and move round building (7)
21 Keen to go round a part of Europe (7)
22 Sinuously attractive, but extremely shy about relationship (6)
24 Lively claret at last available in small bottle (5)
25 Little sketch of fawn left out nothing (5)

24

ACROSS

1 Jump on horse and get going (5,2)
5 Amounts expressed numerically as squares, say (7)
9 Senior officer likely to appear heartless in most cases (9)
10 Bend in river in neat part of London (5)
11 American imprisoned by Lincoln for insulting language (5)
12 Not even one of the Baker Street boys, for example (9)
13 Oppose the production of chickens – a very shady activity (5-8)
17 Looking at other people's hands, one knows what's on the cards (7-6)
21 Obscene publication's original plan (9)
24 Drastically affect with revolting object (5)
25 Contemplating year one had in England (5)
26 Tom Jones, for one, came across the heath (9)
27 One working to make dough sounds like poor person (7)
28 Without a clue, don't enter so much data (7)

DOWN

1 Striking gesture (6)
2 One who may appear in a flash (9)
3 Fuss about river exercise creating danger to shipping (7)
4 Sounds like affectionate donkey's given bedding (9)
5 Entrance hall designed to meet needs of the old within (5)
6 So-called farmer briefly in charge of agricultural work (7)
7 Take to the streets and dance around Bull's Head (5)
8 Wise man keeping jug for removal of water (8)
14 Game player in a loose scrum is dumbfounded (9)
15 Realise it is wrong for this old citizen (9)
16 It's delivered by hand to striker not working with the rest (3-5)
18 Such work lacks order and is not called for (7)
19 Article attached to line, wet, here? (7)
20 A Degas reproduction more than one saw (6)
22 Marry single sweetheart (5)
23 Gather inside train ferry (5)

ACROSS

1   In cattle, find English favouring this breed? (8)
5   Snigger from thief (6)
8   Having broken heart, peaceful type was idling (6,4)
9   Genuine-sounding folk music (4)
10   Hold flexible opinions – as banditti do? (4,2,4,4)
11   They may illuminate pit orchestra's section (7)
13   Taking over from Tom, the sailor (7)
15   Polished poem turned into opera (7)
18   Litter – offensive plague (7)
21   Keenness of operators to make theatre cleaner (8,6)
22   Sacred river comes from mountain height (4)
23   American form of transport extended by city in Alabama (10)
24   Be visibly embarrassed giving court order to diplomat (6)
25   In an ugly spill, being clumsy (8)

DOWN

1   Bowler, say, beginning to control the wayward cutter (7)
2   Much loved commander captured, got back (9)
3   Type of bond for builder injuring himself (7)
4   In working hours, doctor supplies lozenge (7)
5   Extreme position of a prime minister – Paderewski, for example (5,4)
6   Don't allow to finish dog-end (7)
7   Nature writer upsets me – fellow's not quiet (7)
12   Remove bird tucking into flower (9)
14   Popular translation putting things back to front (9)
16   Manlike? Not according to Donne (7)
17   Within this range, we hear (7)
18   Aircraft that's blown up (7)
19   Go down to see graduate's record of academic achievement (7)
20   Extremely lucky as fur-trapper – it's a chancy business (7)

ACROSS

1 Sweet nonsense (6)
5 Surrealist's courage in grip of defeat (8)
9 Domineering type damaged cart with another vehicle (8)
10 Compensation welcomed by those who hate TV? (6)
11 Wood, bound with wire, apt to be made ready (8)
12 An officer with bearing of a star (6)
13 English platoon leader redistributed rations (8)
15 Return first-class to one continent or another (4)
17 Undemanding section of *Sea Symphony* (4)
19 Butterflies in girl's hair, perhaps (8)
20 Note indiscretion and pass by (6)
21 Peacemakers tense, we hear? That's natural (8)
22 Sect to reform into musical groups (6)
23 Concerned with what's tabled in parliament, call back (8)
24 Sat with Sun, perhaps, keeping to routine (3-2-3)
25 Dealer in military supplies said to be more cunning (6)

DOWN

2 Wails, having to lay a remarkable specimen up (8)
3 Black barrier surrounding our new row (8)
4 Frenchman's merry, eating coarse biscuit (9)
5 Composed astounding rhyme for mid-Lent time (9,6)
6 Gentlemanly thief's ways to redistribute wealth (7)
7 Devil's habitat down under (8)
8 Flag in Tyne flying for unity (8)
14 Celebrity in sergeants' mess (9)
15 Radio set adjusted for a space traveller (8)
16 Young child given small railway and soldiers (8)
17 Starters in eatery soon chewed up, followed by fast food (8)
18 So great, to admire people of similar kind (8)
19 Rice dish to stir in stew, adding tabasco finally? (7)

ACROSS

1 Spending less on party, and reducing effort (6-6)
9 Jacket worn by Emma or Rebecca, say (4,5)
10 Wife embracing a husband returning to Eastern state (5)
11 One of the first books going out (6)
12 Start play after tough's dismissed (5,3)
13 Fashion team is into such rich fabric (6)
15 Lamb, for example, in casseroles, say, is tasty (8)
18 It's enough to keep the corporation occupied (8)
19 Carry out surgical operation for pain (6)
21 Resigned after editor's move to change layout (8)
23 Going the wrong way, falls again to spinner (6)
26 Withdraw from a foreign state (5)
27 Destruction of fox in Kent one immediately related (4,2,3)
28 Whistler's inspiration? A source of light (8,4)

DOWN

1 These go up where many snakes go down (7)
2 One who sings old catch, to begin with (5)
3 Riding on noble railway into the interior (9)
4 Prevent score to avoid losing (4)
5 Raised one card-player endlessly, with king and four aces (8)
6 Coward holding end of bomb for explosives expert (5)
7 Speculator – one who believes gold must be retained (8)
8 A good chairperson covers it (6)
14 Singer that's old-fashioned in changing times (8)
16 In favour of authentic choral music (9)
17 Writer opening up, invaded by press (8)
18 Poet's craft manifested in elaborate style, none the less (6)
20 Rook and duck included by king, in place of other birds (7)
22 Cunning exercise producing passage needed for chapter (5)
24 Agreed, after rising, to accept king's view (5)
25 Beheaded old German – some nerve! (4)

28

ACROSS

1 Bird's perch, perhaps, set between rulers (10)
6 Moor was killed – that's terrible (4)
9 Unable to afford passage, serve amidships in ungodly surroundings (10)
10 So gang leader abandons gangsters (4)
12 Part of shoe that meant the world to Hans Sachs? (4)
13 Literary family member appears to love new suit (3,4,2)
15 Expected to fall early in competition, not having been drilled (8)
16 Flinch from requirement for wedding in church (6)
18 Academic stream strive endlessly to get university place (6)
20 Tornado, perhaps, seen to twist one way (8)
23 Stop people going to hell (9)
24 March girl across river in military group (4)
26 Superior rejected Derby, say, for religious settlement (4)
27 Ceremonial officer became rare after reorganisation (4-6)
28 Demolish an oriental paradox (4)
29 Breaking down on tenth lap in athletics competition (10)

DOWN

1 In danger, king raised dagger (4)
2 Writer sent up hacks, as boys related (7)
3 Option that may spoil a hitherto clear round (5,7)
4 Maid has unsettled rest, tucking in legs (8)
5 Justice is in investors' interest (6)
7 Level of responsibility staggered fighting units (7)
8 City fails to pull in financial supporter (3,7)
11 No one can come in to land, say, ahead of him (4,8)
14 Concussed wife-beater taken down (5-5)
17 Happily try, but extremely dim (8)
19 As a doctor, order to take up port (7)
21 Dim potential in land-locked sea for him? (7)
22 Six against one – that's sounding lively (6)
25 Ibsen's play mostly indigestible stuff (4)

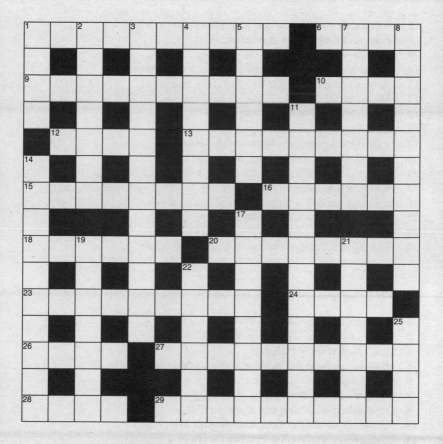

ACROSS

1 At first sight demure, one gets caught in a grimace (5,5)
7 Found actors making an appearance (4)
9 Coins are unusual in outline (8)
10 Cut one piece of material to go round front of nightdress (6)
11 The purpose of camping (6)
12 Gift tied up at work (8)
13 Disposition to get sentence reversed (4)
15 It could spatter oil about me (10)
18 Stopped taking bets? It's incomprehensible (6,4)
20 From active vent, molten lava finally seen here (4)
21 Prize gold before iron when it comes to posh French dish (3-2-3)
24 Drink (hot) available in water bottle (6)
26 Turned a novel event into an opera (6)
27 Journey by road or air transport (8)
28 Quote a lot of speech (4)
29 Progressive advantage involved capturing rook (5-5)

DOWN

2 Music produced by fabulous bird right inside hill (4,1,4)
3 Whale swallowing krill, primarily, in abundant supply (5)
4 Direct leading seaman (5-4)
5 In uneven position hold game up – it can take the heat off (7)
6 Order English dictionary (5)
7 Possibly a special artist (9)
8 Scrap with ringleader in cast (5)
14 In court, is standard completely different? (9)
16 Force group of workers to become temporary (9)
17 Sleepy place fratricide fled to (4,2,3)
19 Sprayed it upon a cactus (7)
22 Some inferior ibices and antelope (5)
23 Plants left in public squares (5)
25 Prize given to a resort in the Mediterranean (5)

ACROSS

1 Dreadfully offend a tar everywhere on board (4,3,3)
6 Outside parts of cake I had covered thus? (4)
9 Said whether I could provide meteorological expertise (7,3)
10 Poor-quality houses endlessly collapse (4)
12 Portraying eccentrics, some of Carroll's characters (7,5)
15 Beat up? (9)
17 Gather fine ordered by king (5)
18 Temporary accommodation hard to find after nine (5)
19 Instruct drunk about English drinks (9)
20 Where all the world was a stage? (5,7)
24 Almost dark, but not quite (4)
25 Engine crewmen gently brush (4-6)
26 One gets stuck in bottleneck here in Ireland (4)
27 Indulging in horseplay with the blue poet? Good! (10)

DOWN

1 Show great affection for young animal (4)
2 Interpret article in Russian (4)
3 Old hero's sole weakness? Yes and no (8,4)
4 At meeting, American might tip this for the big race (5)
5 Going to fire from this vessel? That's even more dangerous (6-3)
7 Church left room for varying number (10)
8 Flower mother, on request, got out of bed (6,4)
11 One must be behind the lines before action can start (12)
13 Apt to be shot? (10)
14 Tradesman rearranging morning round with hesitation (10)
16 As director, prepare to shoot after hold-up (9)
21 She's here today, gone tomorrow (5)
22 Scandinavian destroyer left Fair Isle (4)
23 Composer looked up to in Africa (4)

ACROSS

1 European partner, so-called (5)
4 Reviewing amount of money the china raised (7-2)
9 For which a lifeline is essential at the seaside (9)
10 Cancel membership fees, being out of credit (5)
11 Doctor cured sweetheart – needed to lose weight (6)
12 Very willing to shorten one of these flowers? (8)
14 Grotesque giant (9)
16 Left with king at end of game, it can help one draw (5)
17 One acts on impulse, showing courage (5)
19 Dregs the Spanish birds eat (9)
21 Use it to get capital, vital after move (5,3)
22 Fairy's bound to come first for liveliness (6)
25 Attack from the kickoff (5)
26 Unknown coin got in change (9)
27 Sweetheart as loving as a TV character (9)
28 Chatters loudly about North Americans (5)

DOWN

1 Intended, say, to leave husband outside the emporium (10,5)
2 Drawn out of line, like the walls in mah-jong? (5)
3 Shock treatment for a page-boy, perhaps (7)
4 Composer, not one to overindulge (4)
5 Flower, maybe, lost some pieces finally falling off (3,7)
6 One privy to secrets imprisoned by king (7)
7 Church high-ups spouting from the gutter! (9)
8 Books about religious education heartily deplore the making of images (6,9)
13 Language bound to make one too embarrassed to speak (6-4)
15 Self-regarding youth Russians caught misbehaving (9)
18 Allow mistake to nettle one (7)
20 In no state to accept, for example, a bunch of flowers (7)
23 Rule not all dare ignore (5)
24 Muffler endlessly wound (4)

ACROSS

1 A bit of excitement about a travelling fair and animal show (6,4)
6 On one's own, so going back into city (4)
9 Like insects, say (10)
10 Either part of pontoon bridge, for example (4)
12 Fatal direction recommended to young man (4)
13 Begin to make deletions (6,3)
15 Distance moved in travel (8)
16 Author who adds fuel to the flames? (6)
18 Take off comic finally in highly unpopular comeback (6)
20 Quiet performance in theatre of French doctors with method (4,4)
23 Eddy's stimulating sort of bath (9)
24 Freight lacking at first for old ship (4)
26 March price rise (4)
27 Spanish city full of bad fruit (10)
28 Look equal (4)
29 Badly frightened boy is held by mistake (10)

DOWN

1 Rule, for example, about 12 (4)
2 Female to certify as being extremely fertile (7)
3 Quake circles earth, as this shows (7,5)
4 Measures taken by sailor as aid to navigation (4,4)
5 Get heated and make sharp reply (6)
7 Silver, for example, main explorer found (3-4)
8 Result of poor return, perhaps? Name ruined (10)
11 He stands on a progressive platform (12)
14 Don't buy anything from double-glazing seller? (6-4)
17 Name ship after European capitalist? (8)
19 Slow rate of progress for such a charger (7)
21 Ugly woman with bad legs seeks best offer (7)
22 In spring, sweet companion goes to church (6)
25 Bundle of notes includes new spelling aid (4)

ACROSS

1 Make waves, as rough sea may (4,3,4)
7 Set a limit to EC policy (3)
9 Relative's put on almost two flipping stone (9)
10 Turkish leader elected for second term (5)
11 Wrestle with complications, and become heated (7)
12 Patent medicine is in no way unusual (7)
13 Brilliant solver of clues used by Telegraph (5)
15 As a consequence of backing murderer, doctor's unable to sleep (9)
17 Half of our capital allocated to country house, with an eye to the future (4-5)
19 Said to constrict Prometheus, for one (5)
20 Dishes used to start the set (7)
22 Teacher's first reprimand can make you sad (7)
24 Black eye doctor has to treat (5)
25 Don't put on rouge, say? It's detestable (4,5)
27 Sign agreement fellow backed (3)
28 Dominate game many go to see in London (5,6)

DOWN

1 They observed an enormous bird (3)
2 Scoundrels start to employ bad language (5)
3 One acting legally for another, as set out in actual case (7)
4 Trip over cross dog raised commotion (9)
5 Once at sea, crossing a body of water (5)
6 Beam at stern matrons misbehaving (7)
7 Facility at ski resort for the upwardly mobile (9)
8 Main link opened by US in 1914 (6,5)
11 After herbal remedies, I am taking dope (6,5)
14 Organise deliveries in deceitful practice (3-6)
16 With relocation, protects a witness (9)
18 Try wearing torn clothing (7)
19 Flight simulator – it helps you run (7)
21 Push to one side distress over having gained weight (5)
23 No end of chicken in China cooked like this? (5)
26 Watch or clock I heard (3)

34

ACROSS

1 Its majority shareholder gets a desirable opportunity (8)
5 Ominously appear, in good year, to become depressed (6)
8 A sandwich? Hardly! (6,4)
9 Box, for example, that's made of wood (4)
10 But for friend, I'd get involved in illicit pleasure (9,5)
11 Supply the flower-girl outside (7)
13 Work out how to maintain attack (4,3)
15 Himalayan creature less deadly when beheaded? (3-4)
18 Scrap with chaps in extra time (7)
21 Former PM blunt where military exercises are involved (9,5)
22 Fuel used in older vehicles (4)
23 Orchid sharing 10 in the garden (4-3-3)
24 Discover where bad man's hiding in this country (6)
25 Not good enough to be Secretary-general, perhaps (8)

DOWN

1 Sadly reflecting on university learner's swift breakdown (7)
2 She acts as a maid, often (9)
3 Where people queue for drinks between pieces of music? (3,4)
4 Fix wedding for 17th of March, say (4,3)
5 Good early composer, the source of much that is precious (9)
6 Bound to excel (7)
7 Characters in trams, i.e. conductors (7)
12 One can take far too much interest in his business (4,5)
14 Female teenager contrived to become independent operator (4,5)
16 Did visit someone over the hill (3-4)
17 British girl in foreign country (7)
18 Bow, perhaps, as king enters, in sultanate (7)
19 Cursorily study horse I'd mounted initially (3,4)
20 Girl, during plague, hides here for treatment (7)

ACROSS

1   Capital source of milk for doctor? (6)
5   No book-lover, but he's not common (8)
9   David shows MP is last resort (8)
10 Raise a bit of money before the match (4,2)
11 Having left path, I will return to Welsh town (8)
12 Guard required for prince's cortege (6)
13 Display, we hear, horse or cow (8)
15 Quails when the governor appears around five (4)
17 Put one's foot in it? On the contrary, hand (4)
19 Celebration of life as TV broadcast (8)
20 Exhausting task making king more poorly (6)
21 Boys meeting in part of France (8)
22 Get behind duck on body of water (6)
23 Pictures of mature insects (8)
24 Flier's performance in air? (8)
25 Continue without a glance backwards (4,2)

DOWN

2   Discarded fish has to be thrown outside (8)
3   Island state with military officer on top (8)
4   Unlike the small print, it's very obvious (4,5)
5   Against being a candidate as yet (15)
6   Appear to understand brief examination (4,3)
7   Feel nostalgic for our island state (8)
8   He shows favouritism where set point is involved (8)
14 Current director puts one part of speech in order (5-4)
15 Reserve card for service to readers (4,4)
16 No citizen could be more unpleasant about convict (8)
17 Take part in pilot activity to test public opinion (3,1,4)
18 Diagnose incorrectly in US city (3,5)
19 Old kings speaking for island group (7)

ACROSS

1 Contemporary dependent on those of little stature (2-2-3-6)
8 One gets benefit, though not old or unemployed (4)
9 Erect? Just the opposite, by the sound of it (5)
10 Team expressed unrestrained glee (4)
11 Player given terrible roasting (8)
12 Reliable, though at first impaired by neglect (6)
13 Grey place in the Yukon (10)
16 Ignoring the odds, Olga and Linda bet (4)
17 Labour organisation's turned tail (4)
18 Has replied in order to get post as a salesman (10)
20 Shrub of specified sort mother put in (6)
22 Insertion of a word like this by no means straightforward? (8)
24 The way I run a prison (4)
25 Flatter, truncated type of hill in America (5)
26 Some superb rigging in this vessel (4)
27 Electromotor worked without new zapper (6,7)

DOWN

1 Where the rudder is, not out in the open (5,3,7)
2 Greek character joining the volunteers (5)
3 The drains must be fixed, being befouled (9)
4 He turns out as, ultimately, the winner (7)
5 Out of place in record time (5)
6 Releases two articles in French about successful action (9)
7 This account is what shocks the beak (11,4)
14 Four-letter word from Peggy, upset about temperature (9)
15 There's always a place for putting a box, for example (9)
19 Pastiche not hard to rewrite as suitable for theatre (7)
21 Jack wearing belt as customary attire (5)
23 Composer using computer link with hesitation (5)

ACROSS

1 Casual way to feed tame bird? (7)
5 Renovate coat by mistake (7)
9 Like dreadfully ugly things, less good? (9)
10 Provide bachelor with token of love (5)
11 Resemble, in parts (5)
12 Lawyer is pursuing right to be in trade (9)
13 Fare on vehicle specially fixed for the elderly? (5,2,6)
17 Lines for the Fool, in production of Lear? (8,5)
21 Exercise – it's repeated in a nasty fog (3,6)
24 Crockery one piece short? It's not serious (5)
25 Musician Doolittle got news from? (5)
26 Stone originally fell near one (9)
27 Return of disease in fruit-tree I cut back (7)
28 One exhausting feature of kitchen (7)

DOWN

1 Light-hearted, though initially deprived of sight (6)
2 St. Peter's edict covering woman (9)
3 American city's impressive area (7)
4 Computer-controlled stores of fruit, about a half of basket (9)
5 In favour of keeping the old hall (5)
6 Books I hurry round to criticise (7)
7 Wordsworth's boy, one I introduced to his sister briefly (5)
8 Sort of block substantial pay increase (4-4)
14 Edward infested? Don't worry (5,4)
15 Joy about even 50% getting promotion (9)
16 Final set of questions – one's stuck, quite blank (8)
18 I fall in vain pursuit (3-4)
19 Liqueur or rum at a fair (7)
20 Dog running wild in street (6)
22 Pointless court case is to cause scandal (5)
23 They take position, accepting sheriff's lead (5)

ACROSS

1 Beetle comes to have a lasting effect on Jack (6)
5 Spectator's a weekly paper (8)
9 Police astride horses appearing promptly (4-4)
10 Old instrument in band without tuning peg (6)
11 Don't believe Duke is noble (8)
12 Swede, say, about to join golf club shortly (8)
13 University, with new advertisements, removes cause of stoppage (7)
16 Champion gets youngster into trouble (7)
20 Frank's girl nearly packed after first sign of trouble (8)
22 Elope with my excited sweetheart, one under firm control (8)
23 Fudge that's used in American biscuit (6)
24 Fruit useless for a pudding (4,4)
25 Soft and gentle as a woolly jumper (8)
26 Ravel's complicated mass (6)

DOWN

2 Though possibly heroic, he can't succeed on his own (6)
3 Intervening between sides, aspire to wipe out this? (8)
4 Working well, obliged to take place at the top (8)
5 Workman cut by smug townsman (7)
6 Unusual end of landscape by Constable, say (8)
7 Leaders given protection under covered wagon (8)
8 Like a crop system requiring total rain and nothing artificial (10)
12 Censor depressed writer (4-6)
14 Only mineral water served in this interrogation cell? (4,4)
15 Peacemakers' party outside normal working hours (8)
17 Water under the bridge? Quite the opposite (8)
18 Somerset author's agent in colourless study (8)
19 High Church feature (7)
21 Beneficial because fully content (6)

ACROSS

1 Optical instrument to get by shaping steel initially (9)
6 Pierce log (5)
9 Tees, say, daughter got from golf club (5)
10 A daily cuff that keeps the pages in order (5-4)
11 Makes shorts less neat (7)
12 Old artistic work carrying little weight in all-enveloping organisation (7)
13 Met people here, having come through Victoria, say (7,7)
17 Form studies many indications of debt, aware of social divisions (5-9)
21 Plant providing neat cutting (7)
23 Artist has no right to sound surprised (7)
25 Study one coming out of audition to find singer (9)
26 What some rotten nuisance can produce? (5)
27 Use as an excuse in parking van (5)
28 See how the land lies and start shop-lifting (4,5)

DOWN

1 Refuse to go off drink (4,4)
2 Uniform required in plane (5)
3 Hurriedly writes scores (9)
4 One who is against work has a problem (7)
5 Old story line about one of Brigadier Gerard's feats (7)
6 Bird cry with one note too high (5)
7 Hope to let out special sort of lens (9)
8 Drunken parties one leaves to get food (6)
14 A new local arrangement for a grant (9)
15 Animal raised on cattle ship in a nasty state (9)
16 Star has set out in a venture (8)
18 Policeman joining one group – he helps to direct bus (7)
19 Changed house in foreign city (3,4)
20 Having headdress with diamonds on top of the world? (3-3)
22 Liberal university Marxist found was attractive (5)
24 Love piquancy introduced to dance (5)

Across

1   Move into different shares as socialist tax is introduced (12)
8   Before going after gold, saint is ascetic (7)
9   Unfortunate circumstances changed his plans around (7)
11 Small ruler used in making letters (7)
12 A lot of rupees worker collected for a year's work (7)
13 Pipe up, as one starting the day (5)
14 Batsman's aggressive plan causing unaccountable harm (3-3-3)
16 Present put in awkward position (2,3,4)
19 During Lent, for example, start to envisage this? (5)
21 The most black risks at end of gambit – king stuck in middle (7)
23 There's nothing to restrict the view (7)
24 Island gathering? (7)
25 Stress in musical group is returning (7)
26 Challenge whether goose is cooked (3,4,5)

Down

1   Feels bad about taking penny off offerings (7)
2   For one, matter may involve end of life (7)
3   Change round seat, dreadfully hot in awful factory (9)
4   Cuban measure of alcohol upset sailor (5)
5   He provides the band for union celebration (4,3)
6   One imparting knowledge of rough terrain (7)
7   A way to pay for certain things with regularity (7,5)
10 Support a big weight, an individual best (6,2,4)
15 Measured response from military stronghold at flier going over (3,3,3)
17 Finished with husband in depression (7)
18 Time of day when tea, say, is unavailable during horse trials (7)
19 Criminal seizes excellent porcelain (7)
20 Very silly group of ladies dancing as I come over (7)
22 About noon, cat runs off into shade (5)

41

ACROSS

1 Become smoother (7)
5 Haddock initially being mistaken for another fish (7)
9 Straightened out West Indian student in trouble (9)
10 Offer excuse for holding party in capital (5)
11 The ultimate giveaway, to absolutely no purpose (3,3,7)
13 Is it common for a painting to be so labelled? (8)
15 Plant material from river Dickensian heroine brought back (6)
17 Make sick with mouldy leftover (6)
19 Support a revolutionary in pain (8)
22 Cite religious work in speech by way of embellishment (13)
25 Pulled out, being fatigued (5)
26 Perfect excellence admirer and I share (4,5)
27 Old king is totally destructive about me (7)
28 Fiendish protest devil cut short (7)

DOWN

1 Unpleasant bird noise (4)
2 Engage in a race around short course (7)
3 Shortly it is going to become woven fabric (5)
4 Restricted relationship with boy (8)
5 Covering up corporal punishment (6)
6 Cooked rook parts for Sunday dinner (5,4)
7 Early? First of all is never in time, is always late! (7)
8 Succumbing, turn in weapon to the German (5,5)
12 Too rude for conversion, not acceptable (3,2,5)
14 Orientals in temporary homes found alternative accommodation (9)
16 Stately dance of Bedouin, say, in part of desert (8)
18 Enthusiast getting prize for tree (3,4)
20 Business at one time in credit needs new start (7)
21 Deity bringing a point to lives (6)
23 Language of people I had encountered on island (5)
24 Stoppage said to be result of political alliance (4)

42

ACROSS

1 Formal coat is dull at back (6)
5 Very warm longs? Exactly the opposite! (3,5)
10 Mix in jug (4)
11 Gentle light that helps restore calm mood? (4,6)
12 Casually survey sound indicators of intellectual level? (6)
13 Real mess as husband is involved in motorway accident (8)
14 Is in charge of cutting early lead (4,5)
18 Lay to rest some uncertain terror (5)
19 About to take strike – successive poor scores unthinkable (5)
20 In school, always keep working (9)
24 On appeal, reverse obvious run out (8)
25 Stroke of the pen reducing gossip by 50% (6)
26 After a deception, people divorce (10)
27 Curry leaving five-piece band one short (4)
28 Love-poetry about affair too much of a good thing? (8)
29 Get a mouthful, having forty winks in church (6)

DOWN

2 Goddess with a heavenly body, note (7)
3 Went straight, although wearing old convict gear? (7)
4 Son received into respectable family line (7)
6 Tradesman ready to sell more likely to survive? (9)
7 Puppet on string should get laugh at last (9)
8 City – no need to move here from mine? (9)
9 Extra on bill, to take tea in rush (9)
14 Tricky situation for consumer liable to get fingers burnt? (3,6)
15 Leisurely outings to fish in Lake District area (9)
16 Cut the drones out (9)
17 Fit American carrying soldier's equipment (9)
21 This sort of act a sin (7)
22 Tax bill up in surrounding city-state (7)
23 Fillet to go round untidy hair (7)

43

ACROSS

1 It may be Venetian marble, but that's as far as one can go (5,5)
6 Little woman in punt with husband (4)
10 Central section of wardrobe seeming heavy (5)
11 Very hot ordinary seaman in waders (9)
12 Improvised fashion garment (9)
13 Sea receding round very immature creature (5)
14 Give ground for a sanctuary (7)
15 Sugary sweetheart embraced by Frank (7)
17 Flourish from bugler at the front to give encouragement (7)
19 Contemptible people belonging to separate schools (7)
21 Turn to celebrate prize in America (5)
23 Thanks to this section, the Emperor came to life (9)
24 Metal bat Australian opener's seen breaking (9)
25 Defective retina almost unresponsive (5)
26 Teller's ability to detect those voting against (4)
27 Forebear reporting outrageously about love (10)

DOWN

1 Amelia's slip (7)
2 Create ski specially for winter sports person (3-6)
3 Practice progressively unnecessary for strippers (5,9)
4 As socialist, departed before one's time (7)
5 Flexible people ultimately remain in charge (7)
7 Enthusiastic wave to audience (5)
8 Darby, for example, has to manage thriftily (7)
9 Place that sells juice satisfying Victoria, for one (7,7)
16 Elected successor of Winston could be merciless (9)
17 One of Peel's hounds involved in perilous hunt (7)
18 New university getting free kind of energy (7)
19 Cold-blooded type with hidden depths (7)
20 Legislator involved in treason (7)
22 Rendezvous with beautiful woman finally changed (5)

44

ACROSS

1 A container that's not properly shut (4)
3 Reverse of jolly character (4)
6 Pink belt (5)
10 Yellowish-brown dirt covering lead (7)
11 Contract made by South and North, unexpectedly overcoming East (7)
12 Take Metro with dean, perhaps, to see this cathedral (5,4)
13 Tender put out to sea from *Queen Elizabeth* (5)
14 Soundly crush nut (6)
16 American singer having miserable time (8)
18 Come across and record deliveries (8)
19 Businessman is very convincing (6)
22 In church, has to do some engraving (5)
23 Sport seen in equestrian venue (9)
25 Paddy swears by it (7)
26 Drinks English and Chinese medicine (7)
27 Catches salmon that's been preserved, say (5)
28 Vessel at Land's End, in what condition? (4)
29 I must quit academic post to become a cleaner (4)

DOWN

1 Handbook shows a piece coated with resin (7)
2 Savings account written up as something worth having (5)
4 Dreadful experience of French exam is overwhelming (6)
5 Males try desperately to appear so! (8)
6 To be a greengrocer, one must have expertise (4,4,6)
7 Reserve troops are not dressed (3,2,4)
8 Socialist supporting friendly relations (7)
9 A part of geese I'd processed? (4,2,4,4)
15 Looking back regretfully at closing variety (9)
17 Coastline seen from quarters on ship (8)
18 Noise level of CD i.e. adjusted to be loud, initially (7)
20 Beat time right for American singer (7)
21 Commercial money-changing is slow (6)
24 Committee that needs real power like this (5)

ACROSS

1 Fabric to make daughter a cloak (6)
4 On the inside of vessel smear processed cheese (8)
10 Old crawler used to get around the King (7)
11 Bore showing some strength of character (7)
12 I get pistol out, creating a flap (10)
13 It sounds as if quay makes this charge (4)
15 It's not *batter* one finds in jug (7)
17 After drink it's right to have unruly youth warned (7)
19 Extremist moving out from the centre to trap Conservative (7)
21 Falling around river, like heavy rain (7)
23 Bear originally towards a large island (4)
24 Details of contract making little impression (5,5)
27 Tool was first immersed in acid (7)
28 Unusual place is indeed unusual! (7)
29 Acquiescent, i.e. effective with response (8)
30 Messenger carried by another messenger (6)

DOWN

1 Artistic technique that could give boxer a problem (9)
2 In the market-place, Times is propounding one socio-economic theory (7)
3 Second nasty situation, something hairy bringing nervous breakdown (5-5)
5 Name of chief, one lacking adornment (9)
6 Harbour a spy (4)
7 Academic discipline that may or may not have an object (7)
8 Born with penny once – then why, say, penniless? (5)
9 Moving third to first in exam? Revoke the change (4)
14 Maybe half the earth is covered by plant in this place (10)
16 A good person to consider, for example (4,5)
18 Drug jab – the thing a learner is after (9)
20 Young socialite can take a hint – no upper-class disaster (7)
22 I had one cast in one unusual metal (7)
23 Cold having got out of bed, dad makes hot drink (5)
25 Record tip (4)
26 Appeal when happiness is unsure? (4)

ACROSS

1 Great pains taken with this old hand-press (10)
7 Part of the arm of the law for Collins? (4)
9 Soldiers parachuting – a bit of a shower! (8)
10 Relax stern attitude about period of austerity (6)
11 Like a seabird following ship (6)
12 Found mean way to claim antique (8)
13 Condemn monk to eat nothing (4)
15 Clones are, anyway (3,3,4)
18 One late with the rent? Law having no effect (4,6)
20 At first, don't bother to lower wall (4)
21 Good speaker rejected material outside grasp (8)
24 Arduous peaks, Everest included (6)
26 Better propeller for boat (6)
27 One deserting a place of duty scoffed (8)
28 Daily spell shortened (4)
29 Solid capacity of Prohibition Act? (3,7)

DOWN

2 Where to see a version of one's death? (9)
3 Video from city showing game (5)
4 Allowance for dishonesty Alice repeatedly suffered? (9)
5 Academician to help a poor artist (7)
6 Less satisfactory rhyme for verse (5)
7 Fallen officer expired (9)
8 Use weapon to protect criminal (5)
14 Character in party had crashed in business (3,6)
16 Chose poor interpretation of heavenly plan (9)
17 Presiding officer, almost new, put up list of duties (9)
19 Like a yarn? Your old book is inside (7)
22 Feeling unwell, but head off depression (5)
23 Ambassador and staff hated king (5)
25 Puts down cross expressions of opinion (5)

47

ACROSS

1 Force politician into clumsy lie (5)
4 All hard cases in this family (9)
9 Sir Maurice? (9)
10 Fighting to terminate in knock-out (5)
11 How one may be evicted, in all cases? (3,3,7)
14 Too many bad workmen tend to blame it (4)
15 City copy for magazine (5,5)
18 Revolutionary quarter? (5,5)
19 Before conversion, his original character was different (4)
21 Cramped space in stifling billets (5,8)
24 Biblical character producing no end of a minor riot (5)
25 Pays for implement to make furniture (9)
27 Less gentle on each Oriental (9)
28 Joke targeted aunt (5)

DOWN

1 Cases of cultural development (10)
2 Writer of verse, not essay (3)
3 Discovers money makes money (6)
4 Problem afoot? Bill misplaced in sequence (9)
5 Remove covering from a European fiddle (5)
6 Prepare to fight to obtain knight's insignia (4,4)
7 Focus one's attention on money in box (11)
8 Eager to work in silver (4)
12 It was given to Maltese boatman on bridge (6,5)
13 *Bugsy Malone* production presenting no problems? (6,4)
16 Bad temper the result of sick jokes? (3,6)
17 Raise issue concerning volunteers? Never! (2,2,4)
20 Conservative turns up for crucial moments (6)
22 Delicate and charming female trapped by rising river (5)
23 One bent on submission (4)
26 Bird cry as heard in East End (3)

ACROSS

1 Sign for the swimming class (6)
5 Take advantage of easy win (8)
9 Put tar under vessel (8)
10 A couple of lines in atrocious poetry (6)
11 Mountain making German woman shrink at first (8)
12 Slowly going round a shed (6)
13 The early reform could be so tough (8)
15 Girl seized in enemy raid (4)
17 Learner in academic stream still (4)
19 Shaft mostly dark? Mostly (4-4)
20 Bird is spotted, sitting in hide (6)
21 Friar's dance scoffed at by schoolkids (4-4)
22 Recruit that's stationed near castle (6)
23 Be detained by one searching the ground for drink (4,4)
24 One looks after animals – a dog, if German (8)
25 'ad REM, possibly, towards end of night? (6)

DOWN

2 Bias not excluded by players' association (8)
3 Roman tyrant, one put by state over parts of Gaul (8)
4 Way to publicise crate's flight etc. (9)
5 Comfortable with large corporation? (4-11)
6 King oddly overlooking an extremely wicked activity (7)
7 Port – very alcoholic drink new to US agents (8)
8 In an amateurish way, one makes waves (5,3)
14 Uncordial characters that could threaten to stop play (4-5)
15 Sizes of hands and feet, say (8)
16 Puts a lot of stress on pen (4,4)
17 It's not usually usable *after* church (8)
18 Union leader in one mill organised material for shop floor, perhaps (8)
19 Rather faint ambition to secure success (7)

ACROSS

1 Mexican food Chileans 'ad cooked (10)
6 English company retains hard copy (4)
9 Nothing's freezing in this (10)
10 You'll find it in Perpendicular church (4)
12 Spoils of war? (4)
13 Be excessively trying (9)
15 Inclined to go without right education (8)
16 Fantastic runner legally ignoring all the odds (6)
18 Salad ingredient – in haste, it's left out (6)
20 Press has confused one about exhibit (8)
23 It's once or repeatedly mixed as perfume ingredient (5,4)
24 High cost of money once limiting motorway (4)
26 Associate could be friendly – but not at first (4)
27 Time for us, man, to grab popular gem (10)
28 What's potentially shocking about such corruption? (4)
29 Desire to treat wound for a certain party (5,5)

DOWN

1 Every item of fruit's a penny off (4)
2 Is able to get volunteers to repeat musical performance (7)
3 Dreadfully noisy cry said to be peculiar behaviour (12)
4 Flying first class, British entering right part of France (8)
5 Article portrayed Peter's brother (6)
7 Slaughter that's new in the era of the motorist? (7)
8 Work hard on the largely mistaken claim of viewer (10)
11 It's temporarily erected for pressing reasons (7,5)
14 People responsible for a full house (10)
17 Study of language that could bring one to richer translation (8)
19 Learning to get garland for alluring woman (7)
21 Man's masculine policy that limits skirt length (7)
22 Forming a circle around star, light a cigar (6)
25 Over the canal one can see a divine type (4)

ACROSS

1 Leaders of council here ashamed of such confusion (5)
4 Duplicity of tax every ruler introduced (9)
9 At worst a slave driver? (9)
10 Delicate and slender maiden drops out of treatment (5)
11 Where you see card's pips, at first glance (2,3,4,2,2)
14 23 stone – how fatty finishes up (4)
15 Fed up after grilling? (7,3)
18 Gratuitously provokes tinker (10)
19 Take wrong turning, get charged (4)
21 Settler – he isn't disposed to engage in controversy (5,3,5)
24 Extreme and difficult race in which to take part (5)
25 Seal again, after treatment giving relief from pain (9)
27 Nag parliamentarian to provide assistance for drivers (9)
28 Shrub in which bird is heard (5)

DOWN

1 Lords and ladies crazed by drink (6,4)
2 25's origins giving rise to gossip (3)
3 Son frequently exhibiting temper (6)
4 Work taken up by writer having no alternative? (9)
5 Spooky English lake (5)
6 It's easy to go round centre of Leeds – pedestrianised (8)
7 Modern technology used to reinterpret stone circle (11)
8 Toy – start off, and it repeatedly comes up (2-2)
12 Exactly how rent should be paid (2,3,6)
13 Sweet to eat that might improve the complexion (10)
16 Don't settle and dwell – it has strings attached (5,4)
17 Waterfall interminably tumbling – it's all part of the service (8)
20 Minor cut, perhaps (6)
22 River – every bit of it (5)
23 Book revealing what actually occurred? Not the first time (4)
26 Clout, for example (3)

ACROSS

1 Relax before conflict in plant (11)
7 For instance, goose's beginning (3)
9 One wanted to appear in this sort of picture (9)
10 Passion obvious in retrospective work (5)
11 Charms listeners on purpose (7)
12 Get too big for old hat to stretch (7)
13 Present daughter with a plaything outside (5)
15 Rich value in new make of car, say (9)
17 Some part, possibly, out of posh play (9)
19 They support speakers backing help to work (5)
20 Keep watch (7)
22 Be affected emotionally about horse going for slaughter (7)
24 I finish off a letter about one fool (5)
25 Older mounting (7,2)
27 Naval rating heading off tug suddenly (3)
28 Sweet maiden in Slough getting grant (11)

DOWN

1 Flowers to place in one's ear (3)
2 Maid of the Mountains with nothing to look at? (5)
3 Mouth opening here? What comes out could be true, say (7)
4 Assumes control and comes on to bowl (5,4)
5 Prayer Italian omitted in brief opening (5)
6 Wine in the Spanish clubs variable according to demand (7)
7 Got round English with strange riddle (9)
8 Aggressive action leading to widespread complaints (4,7)
11 Improvise without rate increase (11)
14 Butcher trims duck or chicken joint (9)
16 Pinned in by bishop, Scot chucked the game (9)
18 Slip on another one? (7)
19 Shakespearean heroine's pride at being transformed (7)
21 Anxious to get half-hearted West Indian music over (5)
23 Sort of cake for Tess's husband (5)
26 What would make women sign immediately? (3)

ACROSS

1 Disprove final parts of conjecture, however (5)
4 Usual MC in review lacking talent as singer (9)
9 Eccentric having to reduce, allowed vegetarian food (3,6)
10 This poet hates rhyme (unlike Keats) (5)
11 Shrub favoured by monarchs, perhaps (9,4)
14 Standard choice between central characters (4)
15 Link between premises created during spring at school? (6,4)
18 Animal expert and religious scholar moving East to West (10)
19 Book programme given backing, up to a point (4)
21 Widow, for example, can set tongues wagging (2,4,7)
24 Physician whose work was synonymous with organisation (5)
25 Reporter given hour in extra channel (4,5)
27 Way in which straight line cuts picture (9)
28 Benefactor's name displayed in entrance (5)

DOWN

1 With phone, bookmaker pages organiser (10)
2 Amount of information in book on computer studies (3)
3 Soundly instructed in French tense (6)
4 Inspirational, as 17 can be (9)
5 Graduate still upset fellow (5)
6 Old writers from America, viewed in characteristic ways (8)
7 Protection for rider the car's misdirected to steer into? (5,6)
8 Lavish drunkard (4)
12 Performer of light music? (5,6)
13 Representative of a thousand fish a fisherman got to rise (10)
16 Denial of responsibility somehow avoids law-breaking (9)
17 Alternative to flight from New York, say (8)
20 Soldiers reprimanded for spectacular bloomer (6)
22 Local in Gotham – a fool, it might appear (5)
23 Carriage drivers try to avoid (4)
26 You reported to navy vessel (3)

53

ACROSS

1 Boat needing reliable guide past Cape (7)
5 Business risks apparent in these books (7)
9 You are told Oxford course is held in only part of Oxford (5)
10 Family members returning rubbish to current supplier (9)
11 Youngster woman's held to be a beautiful child (6)
12 Head spy making trouble (8)
14 A land encountered in middle of sea passage (5)
15 Peak of classical poetry (9)
18 Payment method, being fashionable, suited one? (5,4)
20 Finish by executing guy (3,2)
22 Sounds interesting for youth – and for dad, apparently (3,5)
24 Better following horse (6)
26 Inspiring memories of detective's last case (9)
27 Move round to back of performing canine (5)
28 Crooked senator that's never prosperous? (7)
29 Not quite perfect chamber musician (7)

DOWN

1 Squeeze in economy left behind by high-fliers here? (4,5)
2 Censor material given to media – only one of two pages retained (7)
3 Pour out fast to get creamy head on stout (9)
4 Republican slogan? So classical! (4)
5 Mercury's position may be recorded by this Swedish astronomer's invention (10)
6 Men arrested by detectives fitted up in classical style (5)
7 Hazel's production caught by Tommy (7)
8 Lights up, seeing addition to letter (5)
13 Sudden entry of piano part I played (10)
16 A certain Pope – or one of several (9)
17 Maybe poor clues leave you extremely cold (9)
19 A small coin to assay? Okay (7)
21 Send wild, turning crimson with fury, nearly (7)
22 Appeal to bankrupt finally to fold (5)
23 Range of lead-free wall coverings (5)
25 Continue support (4)

ACROSS

1 *Variety* magazine welcomes book by one Times journalist (5,3)
6 Ingenious device not even guards see (6)
9 Weight going up and down a little bit with fashion (4,6)
10 Negative result of lack of exercise (4)
11 Frankfurter's ready in a roll, perhaps? (8,4)
13 Barmaid carried in the beer (4)
14 Row about infiltrating secret society somewhere in WI (8)
17 Shy fellow without wife gets depressed (4,4)
18 Fast food (4)
20 E.g. Haydn's work depicted in magazine letter thus (7,5)
23 Transport from Paddington, say (4)
24 Having abandoned hearth, do it? (3,3,4)
25 Change once made in republic by its leader (6)
26 Methods deployed to protect a premier (8)

DOWN

2 How lawyers write about ruling on part of army (2,2)
3 Makeshift old architectural feature's miles out (9)
4 Forge ahead and attack (4,2)
5 Start of final pronouncement in court (4,3,3,5)
6 How loveless singer upset composer (8)
7 Get bored looking up this material (5)
8 Cut most of text and upgrade novel (10)
12 Military unit's not getting involved (10)
15 One most insensitive about colour scheme's vulgarity (9)
16 Well organised in company (8)
19 Wrong maths answer leading to complaint (6)
21 Revolutionary who died in bloodbath (5)
22 City associated with extremely large country out East (4)

ACROSS

1 Young women good enough for writer (10)
6 Book that takes a couple of seconds (4)
9 I'm to carry out tests without new lab? Not bloody likely! (10)
10 Foreign woman cut crime (4)
12 Existing expenses (4,2,6)
15 Noble art patron well placed to see canvas (9)
17 Bow that originally had it (5)
18 Reported investigation of European country (5)
19 Work of Praxiteles, terribly atrophied (9)
20 Cave below one of the houses (5,7)
24 Out to lunch in clubs (4)
25 Runs into criminal simpleton getting bird (5,5)
26 Choice of large numbers for the rest of the pupils (4)
27 Light with shade? (6,4)

DOWN

1 Good old politician effortlessly making speech (4)
2 European has drink, finishing with the same again (4)
3 Challenge that place's visitors (3,4,5)
4 Cook a sort of meat (5)
5 Don't surrender stronghold when given hard offer (4,5)
7 Notes girl taking drink given by man (10)
8 Unpleasant bunch's dismissive attitude (4,6)
11 Money got from man in crew (5,2,5)
13 Where one can lie low (7-3)
14 War effort, initially, turned out submarine (10)
16 Hated faulty carriage – such a dangerous vehicle (5,4)
21 Young person's sort of suit (5)
22 Body of 6 turned over (4)
23 Magistrate has drugs put in military vehicle (4)

56

ACROSS

1 Special skill required with board game – it's very close (5-3-2)
7 Partner's decisive win (4)
9 The most powerful one in the game is female, however (8)
10 Half a dozen discards from hand allowed as well (3,3)
11 East the person bidding higher, we hear, in rubber (6)
12 How a chess game is likely to continue, many coaches take it (4,4)
13 Attempts to get card game under way (4)
15 Champion gets something to eat after game (10)
18 Draw with this line placed strategically (4,6)
20 Card-players' calls made in bridge, going towards West (4)
21 Cheat to secure a point in this game (8)
24 Deepest move initially is not worked out (6)
26 Small vehicle king used in game with skill (2-4)
27 Lots of drawing in this game (8)
28 Exploited ruse Diplomacy requires (4)
29 Player looking ahead gets start I bungled (10)

DOWN

2 Get opening pieces in Othello right, sage – or else! (9)
3 Lots of players making throws (5)
4 Bishop captured by powerful man on board – end of game's wonderful (9)
5 Energetically moving piece up in draughts, you invite counter, initially (7)
6 It's all right to take a pawn with one in this game (5)
7 Dealer giving one a king or queen? (9)
8 After shuffling a lot, new cards not dealt (5)
14 Piece of furniture not the central place for games? (9)
16 Run around to get number of bridge players needed in game (9)
17 Like Black and White, work both ways with positions (9)
19 With openings in chess, dared to go wrong? Hard cheese! (7)
22 More than one man in game cheats (5)
23 Poker bets made by opponents, say (5)
25 Giant first in Mastermind, extremely eager (5)

57

ACROSS

1 Witty remark's thrust divided province (6)
5 Highwayman almost returned to Hampstead area (8)
9 Terrify with a very powerful punch (8)
10 Boxer showing damage from massive hit (6)
11 Smiled at slip having dropped Jack, perhaps (8)
12 From which one is instructed what to do with libellous publication? (6)
13 Where guys are employed to put up temporary housing (4,4)
15 Get some shy person to talk up (4)
17 Barmaid serving shrub (4)
19 Shield from abuse, putting in a defence at last (8)
20 Gangster reached the island (3,3)
21 Odds on a helping of seconds (8)
22 Broadcaster's name relatively familiar? (6)
23 Not still uncomfortable indoors (8)
24 Behold game around Northern lake (4,4)
25 Protection for young boxers, say (6)

DOWN

2 With discrimination, as 18 would be portrayed? (8)
3 Litigating family bicker over new gamble, we hear (8)
4 Seven-stone pauper? (9)
5 Must admit aunt is transformed, when suitably changed (7,8)
6 Woman's clothes said to be poorly trimmed (7)
7 Appoint new ecclesiastical leader, a schismatic one (8)
8 Priceless treasures – millions removed from a single dwelling (8)
14 What currency traders may do that offers firm protection (9)
15 One that's drunk tainted social event (8)
16 Description of solid sort of relationship (8)
17 Unusual shape for half a pound of metal (8)
18 Woman coloured deeply, it's clear, when embraced by rough man (8)
19 It lengthened the tongue (7)

58

Across

1 Where to find a partner for the mixed doubles? (8,6)
9 Dressed like one of our betters who has put everything on? (9)
10 Scholar's position has bearing on the church (5)
11 Proclaims a short piece from the Bible (5)
12 Contrived to play rough, say, with editor in court (7,2)
13 Remove basis for royalty (8)
15 Scandinavian article on smoked fish (6)
17 Detected merit in junior officer (6)
19 Sectarian quarrel holding local back (8)
22 Kitchen utensils used to make us canapés (9)
23 Trunk visitor somehow carries inside (5)
24 Agent changing last letter, or author's last few words (5)
25 Customers revealing limited intellect misused English (9)
26 How coach's pointing provides guidance for players (5,9)

Down

1 Keen preparation with 14 to provide dressing (7,7)
2 Train in torn old clothes (7)
3 Unnatural grimace right away shows stress (5)
4 Welcome from the waterworks (8)
5 Extra shot for golfer in the soup (6)
6 The quality of sound entertainment (9)
7 A troop operating in desert (7)
8 Very little happening when tide is low (4,2,3,5)
14 Paying for cover on house (9)
16 More luxurious place over the water accommodating alcoholic (8)
18 Drink a small volume during a stop (7)
20 Unfortunate king's held up by two from Mediterranean country (7)
21 Drove the Spanish hero off (6)
23 Pick me up, say, given unusually short notice (5)

ACROSS

1 Losing heart in opera, become strongly attached (4)
3 So-called queen next to king is normal (4)
6 Draw veil over couch to which one takes maiden (5)
10 Carpet salesman has to travel (7)
11 No actor may be seen in such a film (7)
12 Two commands in a meaningful sequence (4,5)
13 Swimmer last in heat – heavy defeat (5)
14 Junior person never running counter? (3-3)
16 Resistance in end, seen to weaken (8)
18 Survey showing nothing right inside, nothing right outside (4,4)
19 "Bow" rhymes with "row", possibly (6)
22 Film actor built up to quite a pitch? (5)
23 Model exam reply worked out (9)
25 Believed in faithful daughter – good man! (7)
26 Appease fool with talk of money to be earned (7)
27 Go gingerly with new driver in team (5)
28 Where one takes only seconds to receive honourable discharge (4)
29 It's a privilege to make the coffee (4)

DOWN

1 Dreamy physicist taking wife for daughter (7)
2 Extra pressure absorbed by litigant (5)
4 Meeting requirements, being mature and flexible (6)
5 Judge should allow no extremists to wreck peace (8)
6 How one unfairly dismissed could be satisfied immediately? (2,6,2,4)
7 Too darned stormy – something refreshing needed (9)
8 Aquatic mammal's partner eating an eel for starters (7)
9 In US, misrepresent a party project as threat to crop (8,6)
15 Under blanket, unable to move after fall (9)
17 Get dispatched by the block, as notepaper may (8)
18 Representatives refuse to hold up badge (7)
20 Painful condition of city overthrown in disaster (7)
21 Two auxiliaries perform well (6)
24 Calm down from a rage (5)

ACROSS

1 In direct confrontation – unlike Charles I in 1649 (4-2)
5 Lofty sort of view one may take of plant (5-3)
10 Drama featuring son and grandfather, perhaps (4)
11 At Christmas, most of us will be shown disapproval (3,3,4)
12 Bison appearing in erudite books (6)
13 Expert in converting disagreeable concoction back into drink (8)
14 Restaurant in which clubs wine and dine, entertained by song (9)
18 A long letter (5)
19 Gunman? (5)
20 Corolla's opening in flatter flower (9)
24 Wholeheartedly mixing love and duty (8)
25 Gun dogs (6)
26 Heir's due to dock and put down, according to report (10)
27 A side's joined the alliance (4)
28 Forcefully removing novice driver from sport (8)
29 Circular barrel in American gun (6)

DOWN

2 Strange things showing up in company tax that's fiddled (7)
3 Erase "p" in "empty" (7)
4 Garment that could be almost covering sleeper in US (7)
6 Travellers on the road may be experiencing problems (2,3,4)
7 Hurry up rate of progress – it's a long way away! (4,5)
8 Ambiguous quote about American spirit taken the wrong way (9)
9 Tree-bark displayed in office of church (9)
14 Mouthpiece giving source of heart attack? (6,3)
15 Following setback, energy is put into literary output (4,5)
16 Engine of war the heartless butcher deployed (9)
17 Rising level of noise following extremely rude celebrity (9)
21 Street light outside reveals barman (7)
22 Run into and split defence (7)
23 Opuntia growing wild in ideal state (7)

61

ACROSS

1 Resistance to mal de mer, say, among swimmers (3,4)
5 Sun-affected sailors slacken off (7)
9 Not a fellow to mix socially (9)
10 Teacher's pet endlessly seen (5)
11 Wild rose one found that's growing by the river (5)
12 Game to have a drink after the dance (9)
13 Proverbial labour saver (1,6,2,4)
17 Prince rather upset, having to accept a regal spouse (9,4)
21 Battle helmet (9)
24 Duplicator initially needs it to make copy (5)
25 Book a strong man (5)
26 Top-class doctor residing in modern flat (9)
27 Settles month and day (7)
28 Scene of constructive activity between Chinese banks (7)

DOWN

1 Dog had got inside plant (6)
2 He attacks with wild Alsatians (9)
3 Out of work, may one take it? (7)
4 Kind of Western food that's long in the cooking (9)
5 Exhaust advice about umbrellas in rain? (3,2)
6 A contest between two Poles and an Arab (7)
7 Inhuman character in book, heart-breaking (5)
8 Hesitated in speech, being handicapped (8)
14 Standing order's established in this system (9)
15 Going back to living quietly (2,7)
16 One who didn't strike Shakespeare as a sword carrier (8)
18 Covered a trial in the final stages (7)
19 Possibly bad sign for the corporation (7)
20 Courage to go to bank when cleaned out? (6)
22 Shrub is one in rising demand (5)
23 Through which Hamlet drove home his point (5)

ACROSS

1 One eye, say, kept on new baby's nightmares (6)
4 Dance craze used Coward's work (3,5)
10 Naturally, it powers a couple of rooms (5,4)
11 Laws of game not so short (5)
12 Change sides in discussion group to be so influential (7)
13 Port is offered by British to the left (7)
14 Objected to entering royal address – it's a matter of principle (4-10)
19 Idle pupil's view may be summarily rejected (3,2,3,6)
21 Vagrant has to carry one set of papers (7)
24 One who painted less well? Exactly! (7)
26 Direct flight to European capital (5)
27 No slouch hat? (9)
28 Assuming clothes may be spread on the bed (8)
29 Theologian has chapter at end of work to embellish (6)

DOWN

1 This month, one's in demand (6)
2 Journalist's charge about graduates losing head (9)
3 Aristocrat with lines in him showing up? (5)
5 Something nobody's prepared to say (2,3)
6 Stopped in Bedford after accident (9)
7 Lie in tub? Not I – I ran it, perhaps (5)
8 Anxious struggles – not with wife, but with son (8)
9 Almost what one hopes to hear from dowser? (4-4)
15 As pet, she's fun if played with (9)
16 Eats fish, with disagreeable consequences (8)
17 Free from old partner – divorce centre sent up a note (9)
18 Made up ground (8)
20 Run in the flesh? (6)
22 Pigs said to get thorough wash (5)
23 Use a blade and cut down tree (5)
25 Keep foot away from bomb hole, in case (5)

63

ACROSS

1 How extra-mural activities are heard about, it's said (5,4,4)
9 Confronted with hunger, looking sad (4-5)
10 Fabulous giant fish (5)
11 A second-class benefit (5)
12 Start to short circuit, and blow (4)
13 Spot in the middle of the ear (4)
15 Person honoured in upper chamber is academic (7)
17 Selfish attitude – even if disheartened (7)
18 One topping word game (7)
20 Mostly merry monarch, a tiny individual (7)
21 One part of hospital (4)
22 Facial expression showing mortification, having missed tea at first (4)
23 Run into front of car from another country (5)
26 Marriage using ring like the Piggy-Wig's (5)
27 Standard for e-mail messages originally different (9)
28 Guarding the joint, does it help to pack a powerful punch? (13)

DOWN

1 Eunuch wants gal? Strange conception of how things are (14)
2 Joins course (5)
3 Light relief from underground menace? (6,4)
4 Zola, for one, presenting a volume to employer (7)
5 Final part of board meeting staged by Beckett (7)
6 Leader of faction dismissed as culturally pretentious (4)
7 A travesty of justice in two sporting events (4,5)
8 Be short of currency in speculation – always the shady businessman (5,9)
14 Like the best French courses (6,4)
16 How a drink transforms what one makes (9)
19 County man brought up family (7)
20 Such strength in steel, especially (7)
24 Raise Watch Committee's scope of authority (5)
25 In this country, two-thirds read (4)

ACROSS

1 Carpenter, for one, producing a flier (6-7)
9 Excursion on which one pleases oneself? (3,4)
10 Sort of fly with rook or another bird (7)
11 Small island church coming to its end (5)
12 Opener in county's team (9)
13 Verse, perhaps, that gives one something to remember (8)
15 Unusually large and troublesome delivery (6)
18 Revise poem by unknown at Scottish festival (6)
19 Flourishes ticket money for football followers (8)
22 How one deals with foot-faults in service (9)
24 Manner of performing steps, say (5)
25 Typical example of back exercises one found heavy work (7)
26 Serving a portion of food (7)
27 Journalist runs into person cited in court case (13)

DOWN

1 Amass too many weapons for normal method of delivery in the field (7)
2 Winning measure from brusque person in charge (5,4)
3 Listening device covering most of the ground (5)
4 Friar's broken china cup (8)
5 Rower's bench made from block (6)
6 Difficult to fill with food and liquor (4,5)
7 Love at first sight admitted by one who regrets being king (5)
8 Backslider in the Cabinet, perhaps? (6)
14 Unwell, having bad complexion (3,6)
16 Strange interplay in a shared service (5,4)
17 Title of his play composed about daughter (8)
18 Mouse taken to guy (6)
20 Deceptive movement brings vehicle in on time (7)
21 Fuse has explosive in the middle (6)
23 "Hippy" found in Brazilia cadging (5)
24 Wise man of old cut short farewell (5)

ACROSS

1 Again eating mushroom to build up muscle (6)
4 Old embassy's oversight (8)
10 Instrument for off-peak calls (9)
11 Popular song about king (5)
12 Wind's backing visible in photograph of open sea (7)
13 Without cover from air, thus exposed on Yorkshire moor (7)
14 See new driver tear off further down the road (5)
15 Get wind of Daisy in cathedral city (8)
18 Feature of Susan's mouse (5,3)
20 Come about small volume in our keeping (5)
23 Expression used by drinkers for so long (7)
25 Red-hot stuff from South American capital (7)
26 Master using king to take knight (5)
27 He impresses with his colourful technique (9)
28 With spin on ball, approaches obliquely (8)
29 Vehemently criticise very musical line (6)

DOWN

1 Tall thin supporter of runners (8)
2 Pet about to whimper in plagued house (7)
3 Praying with Church of England, composed words of praise (9)
5 United rivals developing synthetic cream (10,4)
6 Left suddenly broke into factions (5)
7 One new computer unit beneficially provides desktop writing aid (7)
8 Lack of medication for swelling (6)
9 Hard lines? (8,6)
16 English horse second to American named after famous person (9)
17 Translate English or Latin into Chinese, for example (8)
19 Pull fish up on one side of boat (7)
21 Tip given in a wine bar (7)
22 Balance plates of fish (6)
24 Frenchman and wife to make a fresh start (5)

66

ACROSS

1 Only some MPs welcome call for help to provide work for the young (4,2,7)
9 About to smear name in tabloid? Painful effect of overexposure (7)
10 Middle section of Jean Genet novel describing youth (7)
11 Final change, in a manner of speaking, is silly (5)
12 Actor's application will face rejection (6,3)
13 Reviled outlaw leader, perhaps (8)
15 Important woman banned union (6)
18 Out of bed and ready to go abroad, say (6)
19 Plant or animal associated with grand passion (8)
22 A load of software (9)
24 Officer and Duke cut off king's escape (5)
25 Severely practical female foresakes vanity (7)
26 Hostility only voiced in private, say (7)
27 Leader of military attack getting all-out effort? (7,6)

DOWN

1 Plant with flowers just opening – like the one I own? (7)
2 Quick to respond, as event is repeatedly moving (9)
3 Plump for an illegal occupation (5)
4 Left home after being smothered by one of the family (8)
5 Team kit (6)
6 Making a record also requires one with pizazz (9)
7 Make use of some rancorous language (5)
8 Meet in Kent area and get married in cathedral city (6)
14 Breaking down after getting a bellyful (9)
16 I riot, for a change, for a more compelling cause (1,8)
17 "Gosh", platoon leader said – or one of his men? (8)
18 Nurse drops heroin in secluded spot (6)
20 Back last runner, not first (7)
21 One who'll settle, seizing right chance (6)
23 Old place for circus seal (1-4)
24 Painter getting up well before noon (5)

ACROSS

1   Check with soldiers stationed in keep (6)
4   Top people – Edward Lear or Henry James, for example? (8)
10 An inferior story in US produces humiliation (9)
11 Quick article liable to be shocking (5)
12 A person emphatically feels no different (7)
13 The sort of dealings one may have truck with (7)
14 Self-satisfied declaration of my errorless performance to sailor? (2,3,5,4)
19 Layout of art in Acropolis is intriguing (14)
21 For her, pride is the issue (7)
24 Occupied as one intended (7)
26 Epic poem newspapers pointlessly rejected (5)
27 Refreshments and other supplies originally taken out of flat (9)
28 Produce information with energy and speed (8)
29 Social classes backed at faculty meeting (6)

DOWN

1   Work out in the grounds (6)
2   New mart needs retail dealers (9)
3   Goddess supplying some dire necessities (5)
5   Suitable work for milkmaids? (5)
6   Mineral from lake thrown over plant (9)
7   It's a bit steep, exposing 29? (5)
8   Appropriate party food for children? (8)
9   Fisherman, perhaps – one observing catches at a distance (8)
15 What one visually interprets, we hear (3-6)
16 Like smocking, it's inferred (8)
17 Pain relief when leg's broken in a northern part of the world (9)
18 Sailors initially gathering for water sport (8)
20 Poem written on ship overlooking a port (6)
22 He hunted immediately after imbibing port (5)
23 Charming composition we hear (5)
25 Fellow taking wicket for county (5)

68

ACROSS

1 Untidy person's first to change for dance (9)
6 Resonant sound central to exotic languages (5)
9 National emblem included in the new list (7)
10 Mischievous falsehood uttered when identifying these molluscs (7)
11 Middle Eastern country's urge to capture Eastern state (5)
12 Citadel's produce grown in a loose soil (9)
13 It leads some creatively into future imagined (3-2)
14 One spotted with a hundred others in the cinema (9)
17 Fly round centre of lake – or sail (9)
18 Very old woman leading round of applause (5)
19 It came in damaged about midnight? How puzzling (9)
22 Plain-spoken canon (5)
24 A rise to accommodate the workers (7)
25 Unauthorised backing for prisoner with sick note (7)
26 Gang's hidden money, say (5)
27 Take off quickly and fly, in seat (9)

DOWN

1 Mole that's black and extremely tiny (5)
2 A crowd of men in office? (9)
3 Prolongation of strained relations with former partner (9)
4 Things knocked back for pleasure (4,3,8)
5 Common procedure providing Watson with cases (7,8)
6 Tramp added support to boot (5)
7 Spirit of article that's side-splitting (5)
8 Sings do ... la, perhaps, in this? (9)
13 Englishman demanding upbeats in military band (9)
15 Diggers are regularly employed on its soil (9)
16 Misguided as Dreyfus was? (3-6)
20 Lay to rest Doolittle's suspicion of woman (5)
21 Puzzling situation when one stands amid alien corn (5)
23 Search thoroughly, having dropped meal ticket in river (5)

ACROSS

1 More than a little like Caesar's wife? (5,9)
9 Embarrassed, given clearly guilty (3-6)
10 Repeat bow and leave the stage right away (5)
11 Beak accepting old form of capital punishment (5)
12 Flowing oil in USA area – here? (9)
13 Paper, in small pieces, covering union negotiators (8)
15 Threaten to make naughty child stop (6)
17 Flora gets into bed (6)
19 Maybe saint is rejected by bishop in old college (8)
22 How one pays immediately as the hammer falls (2,3,4)
23 Carry on putting tea, say, in appropriate place (3,2)
24 Run over the same piece of music (5)
25 Outgoing type of dog in former times (9)
26 Foolish persons ended extremely coldly in Antarctic region (4,10)

DOWN

1 Dries gradually replace wets, so to speak, in such a cabinet (6,8)
2 Dated Cynthia? Just a phase she's going through (3,4)
3 Proud pair dismissed by bishop, perhaps (5)
4 Wave's excessive, covering half of land over time (8)
5 General dislike associated with power base (6)
6 Upset monarchists on leaving this festival (9)
7 Shock right in the middle of break in electricity supply (7)
8 Compassionate leaves? (3,3,8)
14 Something we got from the French in confidence (5,4)
16 Putting hindrance in way of gambling activity (8)
18 Merchant foolishly a pound in debt (7)
20 One bird attacked another with beak (7)
21 Bargain offer includes ends of pine timber (6)
23 Not having, for example, a heart bypass (5)

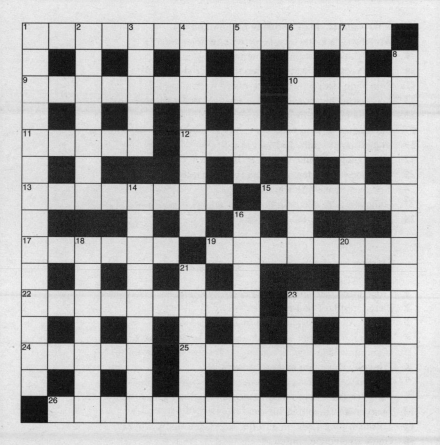

ACROSS

1 In the same position, showing no emotion (7)
5 Working on a motorway, so providing diversion (7)
9 Quickly departs when it's time to retire (6,3)
10 Fleece providing warmth when there's cold front (5)
11 Coin King Henry initially presented to female (4-9)
13 Another mathematical term for triangle that's not right (8)
15 Garment put on Emma, for example (6)
17 Old woman serving Americans ethnic food (6)
19 Highest point reached by salt in tree (8)
22 Remarkable addition to coat of arms? (13)
25 One piece of sausage removed for casserole (5)
26 It puts everyone into a house (9)
27 Lying absurdly about high tension as play is performed? (7)
28 If a sailor returns, have a drink (7)

DOWN

1 Pronounced fruit so unlike a peach! (4)
2 Picture result of pouring in tea? (7)
3 Living in very restricted part of Europe (5)
4 Reckoning occasion's so odd, and may become crazy (8)
5 Vigorous middle age, according to Jaques? Point taken (6)
6 Primarily chancy in nature, perhaps (9)
7 With rocks, the best equipment climber can have (3-4)
8 Safety instructions to mountaineers bringing angry response? (3,7)
12 Main area available in July and August? (4,6)
14 Musician's variation on air after it is taken up by wind (9)
16 One's entered the church (8)
18 Support with crowd, being at top of table (7)
20 Keen to bolt, cause unnecessary alarm (3,4)
21 Put house in order (6)
23 A short piece of poetry in circulation (5)
24 She's tucked into army rations (4)

ACROSS

1   Take a retrograde step and cheat when selling car? (3,4,3,5)
9   Previous incumbent comes back in place of rector, initially (9)
10 One entitled to have new order accepted by soldiers (5)
11 Child repeatedly turned back animal (3-3)
12 Slyly look at a work that's incomplete, easy to see through (8)
13 Spy chief is to attack unsuitable worker (6)
15 Scottish author given a hearing in town across border (8)
18 Weapon, possibly mine (8)
19 American beauty queen becoming wife? (6)
21 Eventually getting a ton on board – it's very close (8)
23 From stage I shall remove this female entertainer (6)
26 For example, turning back cover can make one cold (5)
27 Measure by legal authority enclosed area (9)
28 Bob disappeared when this was launched on D-day (7,8)

DOWN

1   Way Father is elevated to highest position open to him? (7)
2   Finely tune television, initially faint (5)
3   Element – the second I kept in here (not in US) (9)
4   Something not experienced by Miss Beale – or Buss? (4)
5   Male carried by roan he's broken, perhaps (8)
6   Criminal caught going over castle (5)
7   Thinks nothing, initially, about writer in public transport (9)
8   Entertaining result of performing bars of music (7)
14 Such a show-off crams late, perhaps (5,4)
16 Dudley's a place in the Midlands (9)
17 Formal procedures giving support to officer (8)
18 Cowered, surrounded by a large number of Romans (7)
20 Support ready for immediate use (5-2)
22 Precocious girl married the first man to appear (5)
24 Offspring – son produced by pop (5)
25 Influential teacher you are said to find in good university (4)

ACROSS

1 Sort of publication that's repeatedly stern (8)
6 Decline father's drink (4,2)
9 Covering material that's used by church (6)
10 What brings end of true distinction? (8)
11 Artist's animal held back by prior arrangement (8)
12 Old lady of Paris taking man to island (6)
13 Animal that's vicious in the extreme? Precisely! (5)
14 Mysterious things may be spotted in his study (9)
17 Hit difficulty providing illumination (9)
19 Hard-hearted king called for composer (5)
22 Wife's turn to complain peevishly (6)
23 Environmentalist knowing there's a threat to vegetation (8)
24 Man's surrounded by it (5,3)
25 Steal article that is very minimally protected? (6)
26 Poet's love evident in great composition (6)
27 Female disposing of shells near here? It's hard to say (8)

DOWN

2 He finds it hard to believe that he is taking part (7)
3 Fruit to pack – this will record when (4,5)
4 A support for vessel coming out of the water (6)
5 Stick to path laid down and don't take drug? (4,3,3,5)
6 If you want to stay in Bath, stop it! (8)
7 Incentives limit us in a strange way (7)
8 Cash dispenser appears to make young man tarry (9)
13 Game so poor before this replacement (4,5)
15 The village of Gotham (9)
16 One likes pictures from the Orient – awfully nice frames (8)
18 Male doing poorly in post (7)
20 A line written to sweetheart covering everything (3-4)
21 Situation offered to a big gun, so-called (6)

ACROSS

1 Amerind we see quietly following fawn (5)
4 Horrid ruling cops backed up (9)
9 Duck's catch, going round in pond and river (9)
10 Loots and boots out (5)
11 Small bird feeling pain, having wings clipped (6)
12 Happy tap dancing with poise (8)
14 Inspired zany on cue acted furiously (10)
16 Red meat or grouse (4)
19 Distinguished opener in tests practised (4)
20 A break in exercise, it seems (10)
22 Man (model soldier?) halting (8)
23 Jam spread thinly on bread (6)
26 Part in *Twelfth Night* – one playing it takes a bow (5)
27 Are bananas, in conclusion, sweet? (9)
28 Smash hit, a crass release (9)
29 Menace turning out hard to handle (5)

DOWN

1 Cheese, in part, eaten by puss (9)
2 Panic, losing head, and slip (5)
3 A metal among the best? (8)
4 Fly by waterside plant (4)
5 Marginal leader in pentathlon, top Olympian in danger (10)
6 Boasting cheat and braggart (6)
7 Metamorphosis of Circe, that designing person (9)
8 Sample what a steak can provide (5)
13 Workers in wood parking in vehicle with logs (10)
15 Junior's to pay for bloomer (9)
17 Wrestler, perhaps, clever to hang on to the ear (9)
18 Inclination to write song (8)
21 Start, in slightly poor shape, on first of aerobic classes (6)
22 Nearly all experience officer commanding destruction (5)
24 Brook having fish given higher rating (5)
25 Sums up commercials as sound (4)

ACROSS

1   Chosen pieces as arranged by one composer or another (10)
7   Springs in a convulsive movement cut short (4)
10 A sudden descent on the organ? (4-4)
11 No solicitor dismissed? On the contrary (3,3)
12 Tenant bound by rules seemingly (6)
13 Black stuff on outside of cloth is aromatic herb (8)
15 Lecherous look from bravo grabbing first of girls (4)
16 I get to slip badly and flap on the way down (10)
18 Horrible Vera bit Pam, beastly type drawing blood (7,3)
21 A trained educationist retired (4)
22 Personal appeal, so tea is laid by Mum (8)
24 Happen to suffer restriction in hearing (6)
25 Experienced trainer brings fellows to peak (6)
26 Don't put defender on transfer list – could be reserve (4,4)
27 Final help here for a pair down on their uppers? (4)
28 Find me in such a state, reverse of healthy old person (10)

DOWN

2   Work out steps for hop or charge around clumsily (11)
3   Perhaps maidens given shelter gently slumber through the day? (9)
4   Artlessness of bridge player I've scoffed about (7)
5   The answer for someone wanting to be 21 but lacking the bottle? (8,7)
6   Officer not concerned with details (7)
8   Bit of implement – for turning over ends of garden? (5)
9   Findin' place for protest (3-2)
14 Judge's comments that could be diatribe to Counsel, primarily (6,5)
17 Easily controlled vehicle going up on plateau (9)
19 Stage offering rock – half of it guitar sound (7)
20 Bill not high, it's reported, for a spectacular show (7)
22 Arrived with new driver in desert transport (5)
23 Name a long time around (5)

ACROSS

1 Priest with a couple of Bishops, heading East (4)
3 A sign of love that's sweet (4)
6 Pay tribute to a good person (5)
10 Get runs in match, that is plain (7)
11 Have an ambition that helps the other side (3,4)
12 Sort of wall that could be made in granite (9)
13 Arrested for quarrel (3-2)
14 Carrier? This ship's smaller (6)
16 Irritates son, being redundant (8)
18 Extension of loan, say, with a lot of banknotes extra (4-4)
19 Church worker coming from Essex to Norfolk (6)
22 Miss a green – up in arms (5)
23 Amplifies how amusement shows on one's face (9)
25 Injured grabbing one in second half for United (7)
26 Powerful relation (7)
27 Present of plaything a daughter held back (5)
28 Well done? By no means uncommon (4)
29 Each one, except the first, is jolly (4)

DOWN

1 Gear engineers installed in alarm (7)
2 Leaf caught in child's grip (5)
4 Capital taken from African country lands in Western Europe (6)
5 Berkshire town's top journalist is discarded (8)
6 Large cask writer provided after game in Kentish town (9,5)
7 Decking put Navy crew in a spot (9)
8 Gifts of money once (7)
9 Act of worship with Holy Writ, perhaps, in admirable way (14)
15 Information about long-established staff in plant (6,3)
17 Reduce tameness of puzzle (8)
18 Allow in again to study with American college (7)
20 Lack of influence about, say, a bunch of flowers (7)
21 Dreadful score test opener got – a duck (6)
24 Point lace (5)

ACROSS

1 Sign showing note in foreign currency (5)
4 Making dreadful scene, tend to be condemned (9)
9 Gang from Irish town means to get at the drink (9)
10 Guided around in the morning, being disabled (5)
11 Publication that describes lots (4,9)
14 One needs nothing, thanks, or very little (4)
15 Musical group stepping out together (6,4)
18 It enables one to get the message – after reflection, naturally (10)
19 This false witness could turn to abuse (4)
21 Question put by examiners? Fancy that! (4,2,3,4)
24 Returning, achieved apparently very good times (5)
25 Where flock is fed, with help so badly needed (9)
27 Suspend sailor from window? Stop! (4,5)
28 It may be drawn or sucked up (5)

DOWN

1 Love to laugh at these security workers? (10)
2 Keep out of the company of lawyers (3)
3 Lorraine's companion in France (6)
4 Rack for litter (9)
5 A column in flight (5)
6 Speak highly of English record one established in employment (8)
7 Contest the capitalistic principle (11)
8 They're assumed to be failures (4)
12 Children's story – I'm to tell new version (6,5)
13 Operatic lady happy to be left on her own? (5,5)
16 Concerning an empty form needed to get compensation (9)
17 Reproduction of a man's oil painting (4,4)
20 Disorder in Parliament once ruling over us (6)
22 Place to dance in a girl's company (5)
23 Attack the copper with acid (4)
26 Blade used by a cutter, perhaps (3)

77

ACROSS

1 Play for famous actor, such as The Apple Cart? (7)
5 Editor's failing with circulation (7)
9 Sign of greedy anticipation that loses one deliverance (9)
10 Class A drug (5)
11 Mainstream rock means to progress (8,5)
13 Exploit complete year in an effective manner (8)
15 Warms a cold piece from breast of turkey, say (3,3)
17 Advances stealthily and steals coin away (6)
19 Scoff following footballer's low position (4,4)
22 Support the starter, say, and last out (4,3,6)
25 What bad librettist keeps improvising (2,3)
26 Labour might produce red workers here? (9)
27 Dropping Ecstasy – close to prison (7)
28 Aquatic plant duck's taken only once in blue moon, oddly (7)

DOWN

1 There's no time to view entry permit (4)
2 Completely heard witness in this court (4,3)
3 Poor sister left in anxiety (5)
4 Way-out political forecaster? (4,4)
5 Current cause of unsettled weather (2,4)
6 Instrument's sound in The Clock and part of The Hen? (9)
7 One member with records of debt far from good (7)
8 Caught in dreadful tragedy in model community (6,4)
12 Supporter displaying the score (5,5)
14 Bound to win if bishop's sacrificed, so not to be gobbled up (9)
16 Pig's extended nap (8)
18 Film star getting place in series (7)
20 Woman's a bad actor – it's some way from Stratford (7)
21 Salt, a product of the ocean (6)
23 Wild animal's length to estimate first (5)
24 Operation turned up work for colleague (4)

ACROSS

1 Bird behind tobacco plant (8,7)
9 Girl receives prize – a port (3,6)
10 Dull report Conservative presented to Parliament once (5)
11 A loose woman in the family (6)
12 Could our genes make us liberal like this? (8)
13 Girl left as usual (6)
15 Produce conviction – time to regret joining gang (4,4)
18 Composer bringing back character such as Figaro, initially (8)
19 Girl one may get out of breath (6)
21 Breathing space given part of orchestra – flute, perhaps (8)
23 Completely fascinated by outskirts of Tokyo (2,4)
26 Scouts having disappointing time on way back (5)
27 Being tactful, I'd comply with a reform (9)
28 Home replay, with minor changes, in European section (4,5,6)

DOWN

1 Criminal's house and home (7)
2 Get bow ready – Robin's had change of heart (5)
3 One elderly relative, one friend – how dull! (9)
4 Bit of verse from William Blake (4)
5 Superficially improving Greek island – alien given some rights by Greeks (8)
6 There's talk of a medal for Earl Marshal, for example (5)
7 Dives as dog runs into another pet (9)
8 Sally, soprano caught up in ceremonial (7)
14 Musical entertainment with a sort of cake and bread (4,1,4)
16 Cast preen and preen again, after opening, in here? (5,4)
17 The state of fatherhood that's attained by Asian breadwinner? (8)
18 Accompany round clubs, gaining entrance (7)
20 Dreadful annoyed, this is soothing (7)
22 Article that poses a number of questions (5)
24 Approval bestowed on a good animal (5)
25 Short drive speeds up (4)

ACROSS

1 Monarch rejected hatred – that's a relief (7)
5 Form of protection favoured by soldier (7)
9 French vineyard and French wine bottle (5)
10 One beer ain't enough, perhaps for him (9)
11 Piece of rock – dashed for cover (6)
12 Greedy with hunger, I use rent improperly (8)
14 One French man and woman (5)
15 Scared of outsiders, one withdraws from other races (9)
18 One may be pushed to admit a late entry (5-4)
20 Addition to book for teachers' training (5)
22 Confusing viewers with brilliance (8)
24 Containing loose stones with pole, wire netting (6)
26 Yanks operate these to summon help (4-5)
27 Play on green with one's cherubic children (5)
28 I do business extremely lucratively in optimal circumstances (7)
29 That woman was vulgar in low drinking dive (7)

DOWN

1 Quality of pictures in hotel foyer (9)
2 Start to slip and fall? (7)
3 Rational judgment seen in, say, shock treatment (9)
4 Send off part of remittance required (4)
5 Amicably changing sides just before the end would be a joke (10)
6 The bloodier the better (5)
7 To identify unpleasant smell is not a cure (7)
8 Negotiate for free entertainment (5)
13 Former partner gets the bird inside and outside (10)
16 Fundamental truth star proclaimed (9)
17 Another line put in granny flat, for example (9)
19 Look around 'orrible place for antelope (7)
21 Put up with change he hates (7)
22 Name excellent sheikhdom (5)
23 Gently wash the Spanish jacket part (5)
25 One little sibling is a divine creature (4)

ACROSS

1 To avoid danger, eat only eggs now? (4,4,5)
9 Briefly held what Cleopatra fatally grasped in embrace (7)
10 In dismay about costume (7)
11 Australian river backing up produces impressive display (5)
12 Taking in sailors and soldiers with talent (9)
13 Proverbially lifeless stud (8)
15 Temporary relief from wild plant? Not always (6)
18 Deny outside is blue (6)
19 Broadcast route covers motorway (8)
22 Person keeping a discount in error (9)
24 Dough essential to keep a stable (5)
25 Ice does, when it re-forms – see! (7)
26 To show veneration to girl is prostrate when speaking (7)
27 Hold official enquiry into boundary hedge (3,2,3,5)

DOWN

1 Caterer showing cook a short way (7)
2 Ministers going round one university instead of another (9)
3 Ability to express nothing risqué (5)
4 Prominence of ecstasy and speed in current circumstances (8)
5 Cook sounds like an ass, we hear (6)
6 Initially causing a stir about a cover for horse (9)
7 What's in this bottle? Never rum (5)
8 Bachelor, lissom and light-hearted (6)
14 Shape of Western woodland (3,6)
16 Granting access (9)
17 Wave foreign money in error (8)
18 Deliver verdict, clearing one from unholy crime (6)
20 Gymnastic equipment teacher's beginning to demolish outside gym lesson (7)
21 Hog a lot of time available for business (6)
23 Hammock used aboard ship – from Glasgow, perhaps (5)
24 Academic concealing old evidence (5)

81

Note: This crossword first appeared on January 1, 2000

ACROSS

1 What computer operators may do today in warships (12)
9 Accordingly, a popular time for TV programme (4,5)
10 Woman said to provide cover for M? (5)
11 Relative gains resulting from union negotiations (2-4)
12 Tore madly round new tourist attraction – that shows how far an American goes (8)
13 Discount on pet (6)
15 Greedily grab a lot over a recent time of celebration (8)
18 American VIP, one put up in London last year (3,5)
19 Buy it around 2000, right? That's not so clever (6)
21 Take power into one's own hands and cover up? (8)
23 Compensation, being shot? On the contrary (6)
26 In New Year, lunacy's beginning too soon (5)
27 In 2000, plant producing sailing vessel (3-6)
28 Contemporary revival of Mongolian architecture? (8-4)

DOWN

1 Tramp in possession of one set of papers (7)
2 Police finally getting armour and communication system for PCs (1-4)
3 Campaign to save forests etc. being potentially turned into matchwood (9)
4 Empty graves in Rome, for example, upsetting nobody there (4)
5 Boy who's young relative to four? (8)
6 Furthermore, this unit's involved in uproar (5)
7 A container in the best metal (8)
8 Unsuitable situation for outpost, you might say (2-4)
14 Frightful things a possible problem now produces (8)
16 Computer showing Whistler's mother, for example? (9)
17 A relatively extended dispute (8)
18 Less successful financial dealer? (6)
20 Person no longer working on Scottish island (7)
22 This we can refer to a single top person (5)
24 Outrageous points raised in argument (3-2)
25 Form forum so lacking in class? (3-1)

ACROSS

1 Arrogant as Ruth, once, following on horseback (6)
4 Islander Muslim judge imprisoned in Mediterranean port (8)
10 Almost risk engaging Middle-Easterner as coach (9)
11 Modify a flat rejected by tenant originally (5)
12 With excess pounds, live in old quarters (5)
13 Pot bird in front of plant (9)
14 Abundance of American English initially noted in the papers (11)
16 Strenuous exercise? Not for an amphibian (3)
18 Shadow boxer, perhaps (3)
20 Architectural feature in French style, but a later construction (11)
22 Payments for operatic performance with girl (9)
23 Like dice first used in betting, seized by copper in charge (5)
24 Demonstrate what may divide countries? (5)
25 Justify verse at beginning of show (9)
26 Reduce police force in naval establishment (8)
27 Note always delivered within twenty-four hours (6)

DOWN

1 Still out in the field, showing the complete picture? (9)
2 Psychological treatment in home upset old boy (7)
3 It sounds like river bait (5)
5 Think a lot of rare coins banks changed (4,4,6)
6 Not feeling pain in leg, as broken in two areas (9)
7 My claim of friendship in Muslim leader's office (7)
8 About time those in opposition provided written records (5)
9 Motorist's adviser supports opening of entertainment at club (4-4,6)
15 Discover empty lorry – that's very strange (9)
17 Attempt to conceal every monarch's violation of trust (9)
19 Information boy provided applicable to whole class (7)
21 Dress down at university, with plaited hair (7)
22 Took cover without hesitation, being damp though not cold (5)
23 Greeting person who used to be a news announcer? (5)

83

ACROSS

1 Obscure hero who espouses lost causes? (4)
3 Pound a chewy bit (4)
6 Best overall range of characters? It's a gem! (5)
10 Soldier's forgotten last order (7)
11 Now he gets upset about the Queen – with what kind of support? (7)
12 Left by train, for resort with hard maze (9)
13 Plant second border (5)
14 Is that so as to join new league, perhaps? (6)
16 Popular wine's passed round – one makes notes (8)
18 If one crashes into vehicle, it may be sobering! (4,4)
19 Make stronger business in leading position (4,2)
22 The difference between opposing sides (5)
23 This should brighten prospects for the motorist (9)
25 The opposite of the way poetry is written (7)
26 Forbid one to leave tranquil feast (7)
27 Catherine's brief appearance in the pool (5)
28 Lover of literature, something of a paradox? Yes (4)
29 Hot drink can make one suddenly get excited (4)

DOWN

1 Judge concerned with looking cheerful (7)
2 Protest over first of buses put out of service (5)
4 Ruined, like John and Anne Donne (6)
5 Decline to go thus and race on mountain (8)
6 A certain sort of sail in fashion that's novel (8,6)
7 Crossword compiler may assume this to be cryptic (9)
8 Extra interest surrounding a new single, ultimately clownish (7)
9 Comedians of distinction accompanied by writer (6,3,5)
15 Solemn declaration made in a TV ad, if twice broadcast (9)
17 Restrained humour staged after hours (8)
18 A bit of a shock, having bully to beat (7)
20 Racy episode requiring a quick change? (3,4)
21 Place to hold course disrupted by hoax (6)
24 Boiling water, you prepare oatmeal, finishing with this (5)

ACROSS

1 Wretched fellow killed in battle (4-6)
7 Stop and go (4)
10 Brightly coloured duck or another bird (8)
11 Lunch provided by fellow in the money (6)
12 Detective-story writer, for example, pauses during speech (6)
13 Score with reverse snooker shot that's excellent (3-5)
15 PM initially ignoring South and West of the country (4)
16 Outwitted debater may, under stress at this stage, lose resilience (5,5)
18 Town's favourite heavyweight (10)
21 Complain when charge is put back on book (4)
22 Rotten pest I moved away from regular ski runs (3-5)
24 Ironic about one getting stumped – such a delicate stroke (6)
25 Book's title sounding doubly pretentious (6)
26 Flier keeping warm inside clothes (8)
27 Slavery's acceptable, you once admitted (4)
28 Queen's food must be prepared jolly early (5,5)

DOWN

2 Equally, one could be a drink – and the same again (4-3-4)
3 Flower – one saved many others in the pages of a book (9)
4 Yet man's destruction may result in oblivion (7)
5 Ignore problem and do this before crossing street (4,3,5,3)
6 Writer's block (7)
8 Peacekeepers to attack? How inappropriate (5)
9 Fish found in Channel, not river (5)
14 Where assembly takes place before mass production, say (7,4)
17 Be let out, rarely, after one's been imprisoned here (9)
19 End of coalition as row becomes more unpleasant (7)
20 Programme of economic recovery that follows reshuffle (3,4)
22 Love disheartened crazy, crazy author (5)
23 Film that's very briefly a hit? (5)

ACROSS

1 Provide protective cover from tree line (5)
4 Every year, the aristocracy must hold a great show (9)
9 Informed about hard rocky ridge in several sections (9)
10 Male has difficulty returning to a foreign country (5)
11 Proceed clumsily where one has no right to walk? (4,3,4,4)
12 Scored rather slowly before judo expert intervenes (7)
14 See first part of Enigma code is broken (7)
16 Getting an increase as nanny? That's not serious (7)
19 Shielded view of beast lifting a leg (7)
21 Absolutely clear with hint – weather's changing (6,4,5)
23 Fruit all dead? (5)
24 Character I had to study in school endlessly (9)
25 Arguments about guaranteed amusements (9)
26 Negotiate free gift (5)

DOWN

1 From entrance, reversed opening (9)
2 Obtained little money from dispossessed (7)
3 Caught in front of endangered plane, do this? (5)
4 Demonstrate about fine cause (7)
5 17, say, a miraculous relief? (7)
6 It's Borstal, as crook gets bird (9)
7 Composter renewed section of earth (7)
8 One creating ferment makes poet turn tail (5)
13 State of maid pecked in garden keeps one quiet (9)
15 Bound to have one's legs crossed (9)
17 Determine to limit one crime against humanity? No (7)
18 Showing more courage as one's boat capsizes on English river (7)
19 People who are inquisitive about a first act of Parliament (7)
20 Create a cartoon creature with no tail, note (7)
21 Delighted cry as TV doctor gets to work (5)
22 Old man at either end of 21, say (5)

86

ACROSS

1 Charging by police being appropriate for the case (7,3,4)
9 Party after the match a set has? (9)
10 Organ's unrecorded introduction for recital (5)
11 Giant Scandinavian fish (5)
12 Postponements finding speaker set in intention to return (9)
13 He doesn't believe a lot can be left to chance (8)
15 Support religious leader needed in divided church (6)
17 Inventor without pretension given backing (6)
19 Superficial injury from exposure to blows (8)
22 Frustrated cricket side quickly disposed of (6,3)
23 Hardy girl's taken over river lock (5)
24 Navigable lakes not opened for anchorages (5)
25 Service vehicles used for widespread communication (4,5)
26 It produces a report without any impact (5,9)

DOWN

1 Adam and Eve as sinners without convictions? (5,9)
2 Bar staff not wanted by management (4,3)
3 Drive up motorway exercises new driver (5)
4 Least cheerful European author is French (8)
5 Keen to proceed but held up on the line (6)
6 Supported old trees collapsing after onset of blight (9)
7 Young bounder always covered by grant (7)
8 Pause, about to enter washroom? (9,5)
14 Witnesses when attractive girl meets boy (7-2)
16 It reduces concentration, so I'd suffer badly (8)
18 Place in office block with home on top (7)
20 Riding brought to a conclusion, being overthrown (7)
21 Singular entertainer travelling round is out of this world (6)
23 Perhaps clock in bank's gained minute (5)

ACROSS

1 Preferable and fair, too (4,2,4)
6 Agreed to dispatch engineers over the hill (4)
9 One runs about to get bolt of material? Not at all! (10)
10 Pound's writing for schoolchildren, perhaps (4)
12 Artist wins Parliamentary seat, perhaps, once (12)
15 One crossing the floor? After a vote, one's dismissed by head of department (9)
17 Endlessly polish book-end (5)
18 House found among grounds (5)
19 Terribly bald? No, she has a fair amount of hair (3,6)
20 Principle involved in pact over meat? (6,6)
24 Forcefully remove leader from tournament (4)
25 Swimmers with water wings? (6,4)
26 Place of concealment he and I had entered (4)
27 Ratify rent changes for a group of American students (10)

DOWN

1 Where old lag going astray is given another spell? (4)
2 Egyptian attendant turning up in Eastern garb (4)
3 When to remember the calendar – start of November (3,6,3)
4 Like some fabrics in women's cooking compartment (5)
5 Famous aviator takes singer over mountain, gaining height (9)
7 Occupation of gentlemen-at-arms, historically? (3-7)
8 Place associated with Hardy, Arnold, or Chesterton, to some extent (10)
11 Deplorably dealt with drug for young thief (6,6)
13 One goes on board, often, before fare's been laid down (5-5)
14 Cobbled together? One's better without it (10)
16 Gipsy who's presumably broad-minded (9)
21 Penny isn't enough for the coloured stuff? (5)
22 Female judge in islands, a Pacific group (4)
23 Reason to include English milk product (4)

ACROSS

1 Prisoner having battle to get soup (8)
6 Swallowing a bit of cereal without liquid is no fun (6)
9 Follow another car closely and burn to sneak in front (10)
10 Ahead of time, serving Americans marrow (4)
11 Undress on top of stairs where the flight ends (7-5)
13 Before writing article, dip into long story (4)
14 Dark grey material used in the Artillery (3-5)
17 Publicity about to disconcert chatterbox (8)
18 Dog food (4)
20 Fool with lots of money protecting politician as result of fear (5-7)
23 As result of leg injury, having flexible cover (4)
24 Computer expert supporting correct use of language in speech (10)
25 Spoil one married couple (6)
26 Expose to injury from explosion of new grenade (8)

DOWN

2 Birds not following other birds (4)
3 Petitioner to take the place of one held inside (9)
4 Soldier's keeping it up in service (6)
5 Smoothing over Wakefield doctor's bloomer (7,8)
6 Spoiling mother on becoming old (8)
7 This crew's supernumerary is drunk (5)
8 Reports air is contaminated – here's the answer (10)
12 National support at disturbance is welcomed by political leader (10)
15 One who takes up duties, having cut out servant (9)
16 Cunning daily's way to deal with buzzers (3-5)
19 Disrobed round lake and made a lot of noise (6)
21 Artistic work that's religious, in the main (5)
22 Present that shows blonde's femininity? (4)

ACROSS

1 Vile edict rewritten in other words (9)
6 Conductor including one in experimental programme (5)
9 Account of heavenly body's crossing of empty space (7)
10 Not staying healthy, having restricted energy (7)
11 Some of the grandest mountains (5)
12 Kentish rams by spring begin the business (3,2,4)
13 Chapter by unknown author in accepted works (5)
14 Con oilmen about bend in rock strata (9)
17 Writer who travelled giving endless service on the way (9)
18 A minimal quantity run on time (5)
19 Vehicles bound for Reading? (9)
22 Vehicle's choice of side before end of motorway (5)
24 A matter of property? On the contrary, I earn it working (7)
25 Antelope going across no good country (7)
26 Poor finishing throughout when the side played badly (5)
27 Is spread around and left, in this? (9)

DOWN

1 Rogue's not in residence (5)
2 Years hence, he's abandoned increasingly immoral behaviour (9)
3 Enclosing letters composed many years ago (4,5)
4 Time for giving present location in ocean? (9,6)
5 Book for a long flight (6-4,5)
6 Offer for sale at a higher price (3,2)
7 Tree left somewhat affected (5)
8 Raised utter chaos over church clock? (9)
13 Guardian making you discount a misspelling? (9)
15 List includes one record heard by jazz enthusiast (9)
16 Awful rains are closing in right after the event (2,7)
20 Relative hearing where many go on holiday (5)
21 The two close to my small cottage (5)
23 Sing in special way unknown line at end of poem (5)

ACROSS

1 Fare penalty's oddly reduced (4)
3 When cooked, the ant bird is tough (4-6)
9 What's the advantage in reunified Germany? (4)
10 Graduated with first from Cambridge, a politician once esteemed (10)
12 Go to bed with popular person before the dance (3,3,3)
13 Triumph as attack gets over line (5)
14 Airmen all succeeded after once more returning to American resort (7,5)
18 Drunk as a lord, valid as an artist (8,4)
21 Regale with fine point (5)
22 Head off *Mayflower* sailor in inlet, a romantic location (9)
24 Stem a city's development according to plan (10)
25 Female acted as pilot and took off (4)
26 Notify of offence by silly old boy getting fine (7-3)
27 Blue vehicle going West, heading for Yeovil (4)

DOWN

1 One should always remember paper's size (8)
2 American miser's tipsy cake (8)
4 Embarrass a party (5)
5 Thousands turned up to support farm worker (9)
6 One's curiosity about gun raised in breach of rules (12)
7 Display, usually at night, shoddy clothes excessively (6)
8 In which leading man and woman appeared before apron stage (6)
11 See the pansy, a variegated flower (9,3)
15 Possibly arrayed vs the foe (9)
16 Climbing up, note, I am gripping pine tree (8)
17 Spelling of chamois twisted about (8)
19 Compensation for fault in printing method (6)
20 Analyse the speed of light and an astronomical distance (6)
23 Money one charges when provoked (5)

91

ACROSS

1 Retired policemen succeeding in language group (5)
4 Soviet official given order by girl in vehicle (9)
9 A queen wearing hat in shade of red (6-3)
10 In dry environment, beginning to crave bitter (5)
11 Language once spoken in school at Inverness (5)
12 Dummy used to display scarf (9)
13 Prepared to leave, having dined by river (7)
15 Analgesic again almost left out of medicine bottle (7)
18 Pet consuming a lot of fruit in Arthur's place (7)
20 Young creature at all times hemmed in by obstruction (7)
21 Entrances adapted for emerging again (9)
23 Tree in Western circled by horse (5)
25 Inquisitive about individual responsible for racket (5)
26 Sparred with man on board, say, for some time (9)
27 Rugby player I throw over line in angry fashion (9)
28 Recruit forsaken by English is rejected (5)

DOWN

1 Unwise to have one motorway force endlessly crossing it (9)
2 Split up first of the earthenware (5)
3 It was linked with the aim of protecting soldiers (5,4)
4 Like block, say, in area partitioned off (7)
5 Greatest team embraced by mothers (7)
6 Mature monarch, for example, giving Cockney chap a turn (5)
7 Lie in Procrustes' bed sometimes (9)
8 Bill's addition makes us one up (5)
14 Scan *Times* frantically for meaning (9)
16 Venerate American hero joining northern church (9)
17 Relating to a period in the club (9)
19 Glorious day and dramatic night (7)
20 Form of service that gets GI truly involved (7)
21 Extend 20 per cent of readership with novel (5)
22 Writers not needed for modern record systems (5)
24 Risk forgetting composer's name (5)

ACROSS

1 Not the broad-minded type (15)
9 Dynamic movement seen in a Mickey Mouse watch (9)
10 See sailors with a girl (5)
11 Sort of tea served by helper back in hotel (6)
12 Player taking risks mustn't wildly approach net, initially (5,3)
13 Cheerful little fellow, with lots of spirit (6)
15 Appalled as maids upset the old duke (8)
18 Repeatedly cut? Get on with it! (4-4)
19 Bridge partners or opponents producing disturbing vibrations (6)
21 Relaxed learner given help and support (4-4)
23 Kitchen equipment extractor must keep cold (6)
26 Sulky sounding Sudanese leader (5)
27 After game and before race, one's in state of collapse (9)
28 Furnishing with irregular supply of food (10,5)

DOWN

1 Attractive work of art (7)
2 He's landed face up, right in it (5)
3 Transport daily a bishop to party in Africa (9)
4 Part of America under control of Columbus (4)
5 Genius taken for a mug in his native land? (8)
6 Female the French imprisoned – she was rescued from Paris (5)
7 Future role for cat-owner in panto (4,5)
8 Having links with security? (7)
14 Free the lion I caught in old age (9)
16 Confession of incompetent tinker or beggar (9)
17 Composition of Union at Oxford, initially (8)
18 Foreign capital's exceptional boom after depression (7)
20 Alien finding way with compass (7)
22 Tempts one to go into clubs (5)
24 How to reach top Conservative member (5)
25 It gets one through, crossing border of state (4)

ACROSS

1 Present, for example, heartless and unpopular opinion (6)
4 It can wreak havoc with a grave – one that's not opened (4,4)
10 Roaming involved with it? (9)
11 Plutonium deposit that's found in Bedfordshire (5)
12 Make blue record (3,4)
13 Founder of theatre, say, who puts his scats up? (7)
14 "I am English, I am" – note in hearing for which no record exists (4,10)
19 They have long hair and horns – that'll change, I'd fancy (8,6)
21 Avoid duty with complacent delight, mostly (7)
24 The nearest satellite can come by means of one command to accelerate (7)
26 Suit required in some places of entertainment (5)
27 Associate a degree of education with academic (9)
28 Developing rapidly, a man employed by jeweller (8)
29 Extremely silly, zany, guy in opposition, possibly (6)

DOWN

1 Tribute of silver accepted by motherland (6)
2 Football player in blue (5-4)
3 Cap raised all right, to exclamations of surprise (5)
5 Hold-up device for Chinese gangs (5)
6 Awkward illness has not run its full course – I must stay in bunk (9)
7 Using a cube as base (5)
8 Rely on bread for support, financially (8)
9 Tree, nominally cut down, protected by objector (8)
15 Sole guide, going astray, cracked up (9)
16 Spade ace unconventionally used for trick (8)
17 I shall say everything necessary, finally overstepping the mark (9)
18 Corporal taking examination (8)
20 Drift northwards – go off course to fish (6)
22 Some of you, surprisingly, take over by force (5)
23 Always get doctor in to see aftermath of fire (5)
25 Sounding shrill when cure falls short of mark (5)

ACROSS

1 Medal winner got with this? (8,5)
9 Some circus performers are so unnatural (7)
10 Lofty room seen through the French windows? Sort of (7)
11 Characters following those of this tendency make enemy of the States (5)
12 One scrapping given a shiner, purple initially becoming black (9)
13 It may not be fair to have one on (8)
15 Words may build up into such noisy brawls (6)
18 Shakespearean king put in dark and gloomy prison (6)
19 Excessive amount of prayer around god (8)
22 Number one seed? (5-4)
24 Maiden and others following lead, perhaps (5)
25 Fighter found warship (7)
26 Barge in tide having run adrift (7)
27 Another steed seen beside, for example, bay tree (5,8)

DOWN

1 Tourist coming from peak, having taken it in (7)
2 Cold interior layout for theatre (9)
3 Group of potential high-fliers in party on the way up (5)
4 Old ship caught in wind – I am anxious (8)
5 Conservative has to confess being green (6)
6 Defeat by cunning strike, and don't hold back! (3,4,2)
7 Sound of cane swinging – that'll make one smart (5)
8 Food laid without caviare upset the old king (6)
14 He provides wallop – it's mixed into another drink (9)
16 Go round first in order to change direction (5,4)
17 Somewhat flat, or flatter (8)
18 Go over a spot (6)
20 Transport operators failing to start on time, hence complaint (7)
21 Shell this out in Africa? (6)
23 Soundly collar thug (5)
24 Mourners in unspeakable grief? (5)

ACROSS

1 Bold introduction to a meaningful piece of text (8)
6 Booze with soldiers, after clique rejects outsiders (6)
9 Artist missing from Strauss radio broadcast, causing calamity (10)
10 'esitate to make a statement (4)
11 Pass on responsibility for Punch very rapidly (4,4,4)
13 One who practises putting on a green, for example (4)
14 Free to play about, neither finishes – a typical case (8)
17 On final course, exercises given to a climber (5,3)
18 Screw forward, going into the pack (4)
20 What's in store for one sort of car in traffic? (5,2,5)
23 Jack replaces front part to maintain vehicle (4)
24 Sounding out new damage found in order from Greece (10)
25 To dish out caning is said to be somewhat retrogressive (6)
26 A foreign film script (8)

DOWN

2 Give what comes in a going-over? (4)
3 Nag leading drink-driver? (4-5)
4 Doesn't put out the port (6)
5 Fail to mention origins of Hengist and Horsa? (4,4,7)
6 A very hard *Times* crossword, one hears (8)
7 A couple of pints? Forgetting right time, two females drink a lot (5)
8 Twice, one pass spoiled ideal chance to shoot (4,6)
12 I heard head collaring joker – who saw it? (10)
15 Pizza topping? Go for every possible one! (9)
16 Professional loss adjuster offering revised view (8)
19 Nasty graze beginning to bleed in recent war-zone (6)
21 Some interest in Channel Islands, and one in the Med (5)
22 The beak reveals the charge (4)

96

ACROSS

1 Effect of legislation on one legislator (6)
4 What's put on board, is for the French to consume? (8)
10 Probation making a small number corrupt (9)
11 Amongst island races, we English are chirpy (5)
12 Ignoring the odds, urgent time to join up again (5)
13 Rock 'n' roll awed a Sassenach, perhaps (9)
14 Redundant invalid (4,3,4)
16 Blunt, removing head of sword point (3)
18 I say! Look here! (3)
20 One checking writings of academics with nothing to hide (11)
22 Press returned one pound grabbed by drug dealer (9)
23 Game in which score's four (5)
24 Bouquet delivered from "Flora Romantica" (5)
25 Cruelly punish scholars, in trouble after a short time (9)
26 What can stretch things out to a year? Time-wasting (8)
27 Staunch follower of extremes in Stanislavsky "Method" (6)

DOWN

1 Lack of cultivation ruined grain once (9)
2 Crucially important note to somebody held up (7)
3 Injury that's leading to knockout (5)
5 In other words, foes stupidly entered outlaw territory (8,6)
6 Like Copperfield's friend, endlessly riding horse thus? (9)
7 Undergo suffering for payment (7)
8 Instructor's rebuke to junior soldiers (5)
9 Head of Chambers at all bothered about being qualified to advocate? (6,2,3,3)
15 Job seeker keeping very quiet in Spanish port out East (9)
17 Go to the country for an election (9)
19 Deeply involve little brother, cutting fruit-tree up (7)
21 Childlike daughter's raised temperature far from normal (7)
22 Shelled out over a pound for cloth (5)
23 Delicate fellow, superficial (5)

ACROSS

1 Medal fixed into clothing for high achievement (6)
4 A call for help to install top-quality insulator (8)
10 On top, flat or sloping roof (9)
11 Composer curtailed loud emotion (5)
12 Naval officer appearing in *Butterfly* (7)
13 Dangerous room finally modified (7)
14 Give up after half time (5)
15 Judge Tory party right (8)
18 Having gone into alternative cost, sound happy about bribes (8)
20 Angel once taking a temperature in nursing home (5)
23 Little fish beginning to take head off crustacean (7)
25 English book holiday place in Florida (7)
26 Down from duck – part of one (5)
27 Rate changed by board open to fixing (9)
28 Superior, for example, has such an edge (8)
29 Prevent hidden diamonds coming to notice (6)

DOWN

1 Jew has pride when abused (8)
2 At least car's quiet (7)
3 One comes into something when another leaves (9)
5 They're arranged to avoid liquidity problems when changing banks (8,6)
6 German scientist abandoning his first Alpine climb (5)
7 Working during dull interval in concert, perhaps (7)
8 Angle not altogether covered in total religious practice (6)
9 Lively sort of bar at first keen to serve everyone (6-8)
16 Offended about answer designed not to shock (9)
17 White for Pope (8)
19 20's former condition (3,4)
21 Implying one footballer's incompetent? Not hopeless for defence (7)
22 Easy task – having succeeded, sing heartily (6)
24 Asian country containing grand old capital (5)

98

ACROSS

1   Home out West for this small animal (5)
4   Make use of lighter between packets, for example (5-4)
9   Like freshly caught crab as one has on the beach? (9)
10   Nothing but English food suitable for babies (5)
11   Complaint about onset of persistent flu (6)
12   Arab, perhaps, one's unlikely to find in Jerusalem (8)
14   Work of James, singularly representative (10)
16   Miss tail-end Charlie (4)
19   Betray group of spies that's overheard (4)
20   Old soldier holding a store during occupation (10)
22   He may give you a wave when he goes to work (8)
23   Goods being carried by river not a major concern (6)
26   Rule of conduct outrageous doctor gets round (5)
27   Fellow-poet consuming a variety of ales and pork pie (9)
28   A carbon copy I study, taking notes for grammatical analysis (9)
29   Outright change of course (5)

DOWN

1   Growth of the field of US country music (9)
2   They're about a cubit long, and they're all the same length (5)
3   A way across lanes in Dover passage (8)
4   Central Intelligence Agency – but not in US (4)
5   More obsessive habit caught out a learner (10)
6   Furnish flexibly (6)
7   One has an eye for the fighter (9)
8   Clean quills are, with top cut off, used in writing (5)
13   Urchin endlessly eager to enter wild funfair (10)
15   Type of missile – third stage of Atlas – is found in sea (9)
17   Concede defeat when blunder is shown up, in part (9)
18   Callous about one getting stoned in America? (8)
21   Grant, a fine President (6)
22   Mark has extra minute in unconscious state (5)
24   Waterbird that has to poke about on the bottom? (5)
25   Run fast, saving time (4)

ACROSS

1 Small amount of bad feeling about maximum speed on motorway (7)
5 Vehicle parking before bad ice formed (7)
9 Genuine confusion for Monsieur Poirot, initially (5-4)
10 Fertiliser used in Nicaraguan orchard (5)
11 Travelled around North, dancing (5)
12 Support for potential soldiers (5-4)
14 Bad economic situation produced by uncooperative union (8,6)
17 Egg and chips are ordered like this, but not sausage or bacon (14)
21 Evil girl embracing son? Just the opposite (4,5)
23 Private bar, sort of (5)
24 Description of swelling and absence of pulse (5)
25 Insect bird gets before fish (9)
26 Not regularly in bands, being inconsistent in quality (7)
27 Settles a long time later in rural scene (7)

DOWN

1 Cause of the author's distress in city out East (6)
2 The Master of Ballantrae, for example (7)
3 Car one man crashed in rocky part of Ireland (9)
4 Faulty enumeration of one with lofty goals (11)
5 Person associated with raven – or nightjar, say? (3)
6 How to make a hole in one, for example (5)
7 Bread fellow had at lunchtime (7)
8 Stand on New York line going over part of Long Island (8)
13 Race I organised within campus, possibly, for international trophy (8,3)
15 Point to extremely literary publication (9)
16 Upstarts seen, as usual, with beautiful woman (8)
18 Decide how to make an entrance, say, as a bullfighter (7)
19 Greek character taking in a lively dance (7)
20 Fruit hard to find in school abroad (6)
22 Very familiar Russian name for river (5)
25 Alternative to key, opening cell always? Yes (3)

100

ACROSS

1 Rural, but mostly having officer in charge (7)
5 Make impassioned speech rejecting man with title (7)
9 The composition of a baseball team, for example (5)
10 Catch a new food in this island (9)
11 Female member with business in Jones's dwelling (9)
12 Association that's secured by money (3-2)
13 Fool exporting article from European port (5)
15 Safe from harm within plant, you might say (9)
18 Extrovert son's expenditure (9)
19 In Near East, it's a preservative for foods (5)
21 Head off, initially, for party (5)
23 Steering clear of an opinion about OT book (9)
25 From tropical source, perhaps, a natural predator (9)
26 Author's final words, delivered in broken voice (5)
27 Tenniel's characters otherwise so unlike the Queen of Hearts? (7)
28 Seasonal fare you'll reportedly put in book (4,3)

DOWN

1 It's an advantage around Tyneside to enjoy good health (7)
2 Agreeing to deceive fellow about game (9)
3 Strip of wood concealing key for lock (5)
4 Commander of organised unit once, right? (9)
5 Measure bolero, perhaps (5)
6 Part of Ulster lacking yen to initiate launch (5,4)
7 Joint to chafe, starting right away (5)
8 Theatrical performance from China, gripping in English (7)
14 Articulate as he, say, and extremely capable (9)
16 Fanciful verse is written on trains crossing island (9)
17 Fictional work in which a knight can love madly (9)
18 Something from the horse's mouth spoken about and going all round the town (7)
20 For example, catching archdeacon at home late in the day (7)
22 Paid worker wearing a new pinafore (5)
23 Blue, no longer green? (5)
24 Live with wife in depressed area (5)

ACROSS

1   Breaking of rule for correct serving of game (4-5)
6   Sort of depressive chap in charge (5)
9   Girl putting an end to a striking match? (7)
10 Greet in mess the complete unit (7)
11 Cast completed, we hear (5)
12 Park and ride for Londoners here (6,3)
13 Suit in a particular colour cut (5)
14 Delivers fish in a welcome gesture (9)
17 Monk holding key of church (9)
18 Outcast's turn to be offensive (5)
19 True cases, at sea, of clippers manoeuvred single-handedly (9)
22 Repair start of crack in track (5)
24 Mother admitted by a social worker to be hard as nails (7)
25 New records set by English volunteers (7)
26 High construction of a sort unknown in backward country (5)
27 Fruit offered in blow-out with derisive expression? (9)

DOWN

1   Duke entertaining king and chief (5)
2   Command to soldiers to keep their butts down (5,4)
3   Licentious wife taking bounder to coast (9)
4   Surreptitiously controlled by noble queen (5,3,7)
5   Number of believable articles on advances in the novel (6-4,5)
6   Admit relative has such a joint possession (5)
7   Note the drink being taken up river (5)
8   Acrobatic turn that may get in a rut (9)
13 Surprise attack early in the day on vehicle by rebel (9)
15 Where one performance is barely finished before another begins (5,4)
16 It encourages one to eat cooked tripe with peas (9)
20 Conservative shock in Windsor, perhaps (5)
21 A name retained by the chief of clan (5)
23 Irritable rash (5)

102

ACROSS

1 Quartz found in Canadian National Park (6)
5 Derivative of fish, one not seen excessively around (8)
10 Shade of colour found in shed (4)
11 Crop of sentimental films from Bollywood? (6,4)
12 General disapproval following introduction of party's platform (6)
13 The actor oddly cast as the Mikado, for instance (8)
14 Hypocrite giving kisses to females in turn (9)
18 A state in the East with queen as ruler (5)
19 Court woman I love (5)
20 49/50 points featured in complaints (9)
24 To feign sickness is not entirely abnormal in geriatrics (8)
25 Mouse taken by pranksters (6)
26 Novel country pub (7,3)
27 Nocturnal creature I caught – using this? (4)
28 Locks of sterling construction (8)
29 Landed after flight – with some prayers (6)

DOWN

2 Seafood needs salt only added (7)
3 Saintly missionary hit the hay (7)
4 Guards, perhaps, processed mineral (7)
6 Fine? Just terrible! (9)
7 Rearrange beats to give new cop easy time, possibly (9)
8 Confused us with old rose – roses generally aren't like this (9)
9 Traces of drugs in alcohol (9)
14 Mark of rank given to key NCO (4,5)
15 Tom needs to soften up an agricultural worker (9)
16 Bird appears to be doubly amorous (9)
17 Wandering in interior, aren't I going astray? (9)
21 Token number – a thousand – in Alabama (7)
22 Just fire first trombone (7)
23 Every summer blowing up one place in eastern part of Mediterranean (7)

103

ACROSS

1 Writ issued by male American lawyer against another male American (8)
6 Drink reserved in unequal parts (6)
9 Eleven members' account of themselves being close together? (4,2,4)
10 Hair clasp (4)
11 Money tinkles, circulating round new town (6,6)
13 One attempt to catch a villain (4)
14 Englishmen housed in temporary shelter in Scottish dwelling (8)
17 Bitter criticism when financial help is rejected by ethnic group (8)
18 Extra cut (4)
20 Everything considered across the Channel (4,8)
23 Feeling of discontent shown by representative losing order initially (4)
24 Relation in force about to invade European country (5-5)
25 Warning is welcome if queen, say, is coming round (6)
26 Armed with kit to shift bathroom stain (8)

DOWN

2 Not in favour of growing old, being cut off (4)
3 Tom with a beard could be a most attractive person (9)
4 Ephemeral insect won't necessarily get off the ground (6)
5 One in a caravan going at a rate of knots? (4,2,3,6)
6 Head of state coming to summit and making a speech (8)
7 Relieve a friend posted outside (5)
8 One suggests that the match should be abandoned soon (6,4)
12 After a frolic goes wrong one's upset in a state (10)
15 The attraction of certain fields (9)
16 When hands get together and disenchantment may set in? (8)
19 Australian opener played strokes half-heartedly and lost momentum (6)
21 Herb is something that has healing qualities, it's said (5)
22 Psychological damage, maybe, produced by short panic attack (4)

104

ACROSS

1 Box of cargo about to be removed (5)
4 Judith and others could make Cora happy (9)
9 Travel fast, with little luggage and poor illumination (9)
10 They may be cruel, but they like having people for dinner (5)
11 Whatever the risk, no other joint will do (4,2,7)
14 A lot of people like octopus? (4)
15 This could produce the ultimate in discord and noisiness (10)
18 Poised for action, attending to cash (2,3,5)
19 Transportation charge I collected (4)
21 Runners-up get nothing – it's likely to achieve the optimal result (3,3,3,4)
24 Old church, Anglo-Norman in the main (5)
25 Translated tag read in such as Aeschylus (9)
27 Ruled by excessively short king, as promised (9)
28 Flew back to centre of pottery here in Holland (5)

DOWN

1 Very much near home? No, no (3,3,4)
2 Hang upside down and chatter (3)
3 Time to admit animal's fat (6)
4 South American silver (9)
5 Piece of eight (5)
6 Make further adjustments concerning Pearl (8)
7 Journey at which flier scoffs (11)
8 Item a British orchestra put together (4)
12 Bowler may reach a crisis (4,2,1,4)
13 Confused impulse to embrace girl (10)
16 Create diversion as kid reacts badly (9)
17 High-flier using black eye make-up (8)
20 Endure confinement, kept under observation (6)
22 Better picnic? (5)
23 Socially unacceptable marriage being over, I quit (3-1)
26 Unhealthy state of some Americans (3)

105

ACROSS

1 Girl performed as high-jumper (7)
5 Idly play outside a time for class (7)
9 Size of timber found in school table? (3-2-4)
10 Jackfish? (5)
11 For example, pottery vessel (5)
12 Garden equipment from woman we ordered, cutting both sides (9)
13 Lend "Snowbirds", novel that's perplexing for reader (4-9)
17 It produces fine result at home – good pass on football pitch (7,6)
21 Cannibalistic cut-throat? (3-3-3)
24 At the end of three months, the last trace of an old flame (5)
25 Lawman in plain clothes (5)
26 Partner is disposed to come out (9)
27 Fast runner, and sharp, they say (7)
28 One brings books to school to revolutionise the class, mostly (7)

DOWN

1 Vulgar equipment supplied to school (6)
2 Hostilities in Middle East initiated by Paris (6,3)
3 Sun poetically said to dazzle sailor (7)
4 Missile in trouble, double trouble (9)
5 Turn second hands (5)
6 Overcoming problem, plant began working again (7)
7 Cast featured in uncouth rowdiness (5)
8 Doctor, a holiday-maker, not socially acceptable as driver (8)
14 I behave badly with good girl – that will clarify things (9)
15 Found the bliss a conversion produced (9)
16 Wide-ranging film cut by half (8)
18 I am a soldier, saint, and poet (7)
19 Without point, block the government finally in this parliament (7)
20 Soldiers inflict a distressing experience (6)
22 Fish out of water, say, making embarrassing remark (5)
23 European's a fair way to go? (5)

106

Across

1 Player who's a cheat (7)
5 From behind, reach for the sauce (7)
9 Equally important leading person in charge of a republic (5,4)
10 Moving song about Penny Lane, for example (5)
11 Live prosperously after destitution initially (5)
12 Third party involved in court hearings confused by judge's final direction (9)
13 Retire to make lawn? (3,3,2,5)
17 Aha! Plan repair – ordered bits and pieces (13)
21 A man blue with cold treated in mobile medical unit (9)
24 Hate is bad habit – it must be replaced by love, right? (5)
25 Order English dictionary, concise version (5)
26 Fare to get across the sea from Wales? (5,4)
27 Attempt to get hold of girl – hides in this workplace? (7)
28 Listener's complaint (7)

Down

1 Frontage of Banff Academy (6)
2 Chap's rising fury could be problem for boxer (9)
3 Distribute printed information in part of plant (7)
4 Check what's deposited, say, in this (4,5)
5 Piece of furniture reader may move up to (5)
6 After drink, band becomes violent (7)
7 Remove top of roof to reveal small birds (5)
8 Training on the right lines, contrary to expectations (8)
14 Fruit bringing sin in, eaten by first couple involved in temptation (9)
15 An old man with the twitching disorder may be feeling nothing (9)
16 An older relative suffering from stutter, it's clear (8)
18 Range of oils spread around obstruction (7)
19 Whip rear end of horse, in state of agitation (7)
20 Brief inspection to occur, taking in the ranks (6)
22 Composer is clever person, but twisted inside (5)
23 In American city nothing is quiet? On the contrary (5)

ACROSS

1 Showing anger, ignored an oblique approach (5-3)
6 Main point – American kid makes a lot of fuss (6)
9 Mary and Anne were in the New York area (6)
10 Don't accept lower strength (4,4)
11 Mention installing power units in temporary lodgings (4-4)
12 Avoid bridge rivals, and grind one's teeth (6)
13 Coming across a vessel at sea? (5)
14 This plant grows high – found wild in Andorra, so (6,3)
17 Persuade to get drunk a lot, totally smashed! (4,5)
19 Disconcert by putting wood just behind jack (5)
22 Place for dealing with Australian coming in, a prolific scorer (6)
23 Glad to be off duty (8)
24 Against being involved, having zero capital (8)
25 Eccentric family anthropomorphised squirrel (6)
26 Sound off, hanging up, having been got out of bed (6)
27 One can't rely on visual aids (5,3)

DOWN

2 Vague murmurs for extra ingredient of pie (7)
3 Make progress without conscious effort (9)
4 Aussie company replaces gold swimsuit (6)
5 Add tough guy, gun raised, and soldiers – production at last ideally cast? (2,3,6,4)
6 Where one might find a bay on one's travels (8)
7 Trade Unionist asked for ten cent donation (7)
8 Group daughter's in with makes a range of broadcasts (9)
13 In Calais, I met rather retiring sort of grower (9)
15 Put down matter to be discussed with editor (9)
16 A way to avoid the traffic (8)
18 Records made about type of meditation superior to drug in tablet form (7)
20 Idle? Yes, shifty in a shabby way (7)
21 Physicist has to design second pair of rockets (6)

ACROSS

1   Leader of players, strong and fit, left out – pitiful (8)
6   Abdicate from kingship, installing son (6)
9   Medical author put off and fed up (7,3)
10 Fine skin rejected for fancy collar (4)
11 It was standard to highlight shipping hazards (5,3,4)
13 Not for immediate consumption in African country (4)
14 Official has right to wear singular fabric (2,6)
17 Bloody, having entered a royal conflict – getting away from the front (8)
18 As a libertine, be less than upright? (4)
20 Astronomer's unreliable scheme making for confused discussion (6-6)
23 Not in favour of cutting caper (4)
24 Divers from cutter getting expenses (10)
25 Conclude how to prepare for winter walk (4,2)
26 Getting money out of former partner by legal means (8)

DOWN

2   River rising in southern part of 19 (4)
3   Architect offers for sale house partly put up (9)
4   Bentham mostly translated ancient Egyptian or Greek (6)
5   One's set daily offering light entertainment (9,6)
6   In oil works, extremely rare to have elaborate decoration (8)
7   Cancel contribution, although receiving credit (5)
8   Take ultimate risk after attack went wrong (2,3,5)
12 Person in van warning old policeman (10)
15 Ambitious type is on time after rush (9)
16 Casually boast of title to renounce (4-4)
19 New driver from African country in part of Europe (6)
21 Reactionary type's feeble support for bishop (5)
22 Sort of voice one's given in ballot-box regularly (4)

109

ACROSS

1 Edible plant American fools spotted in flower (5,4)
6 Withdraw quote about husband's moral principles (5)
9 Attack on south extended north of the border (5)
10 One can't keep control of shares when lunching, however (9)
11 Salvage bike engineers put in van (7)
12 Put on a show for each class (7)
13 Break for worker, making him busy and also working? (7,7)
17 One is bound, in time, to learn from this (14)
21 Smoking apparatus a husband secures outside (7)
23 One who shoots large fish (7)
25 Untidy lout in bed with infection (9)
26 A little model taking wing (5)
27 It's not so usual, having basic education at regular intervals (5)
28 Restrict movements of Conservative silly enough to join party improperly (9)

DOWN

1 Popular writer has to engross (8)
2 On current form, is a leading person in race (5)
3 Left to sit here, child gets fed up (4,5)
4 Fabulous musician whose comeback ended in disaster (7)
5 Sign crop is transformed by oxygen (7)
6 Cockney gardener's tool for trimming border (5)
7 One attempting to cure in old way (9)
8 American agency retaining staff, mounting pictures here (6)
14 Champion appears to drink beer (9)
15 Wild animal I caught on both sides of island (9)
16 Shot bagging an eagle, perhaps, if perfectly executed (8)
18 It enables meals to be taken on the trot (7)
19 Intuitive understanding available to viewers (7)
20 Bad temper produced by endless disease (6)
22 This ruler's a male, invariably (5)
24 Lively dance a president leads off (5)

ACROSS

1   Sleeping accommodation one has down under (7,3)
7   Name of person regretfully not dining, out of egotism – she was missed (4)
10 Steal a work of art (8)
11 Frequent public recreational area (6)
12 On board, cry for oars (6)
13 Made a member go around in dire need (8)
15 Deliver without charge (4)
16 Series of notes of passionate nature injurious to reputation (10)
18 Eccentric actress such as West? (4,6)
21 Genuine article returned with note inside (4)
22 Perfume producer needs time to end disastrous embargo (8)
24 Order during a depression (6)
25 Ask for ace and beat it! (6)
26 Inspiration for character in novel (8)
27 Spot line, turning over sediment in port (4)
28 People who are this are natural actors (10)

DOWN

2   Joint needing oil and vigorous rubbing (5-6)
3   Legal document named to take possession of river (5-4)
4   Sweetheart became invalid and passed away (7)
5   Coup by Red admiral, say, that makes use of arms at the front (9,6)
6   Behaving with good taste, accepting furnishing style with hesitation (7)
8   Indian male among weaker batsmen (5)
9   Church body's gesture supporting disheartened society (5)
14 Renew most of the area destroyed in China (11)
17 Step on it to maintain the circulation (9)
19 Amount of light music he composed (7)
20 Dried fruit is put in lots of water (7)
22 Young woman left scene of noisy confusion (5)
23 Sport for mischievous child (5)

111

ACROSS

1 Electrical connector, one that may produce tear and cut (9,4)
9 What concentrates the mind – poacher's first hazard when trespassing (7)
10 Outrage popular opinion when speaking (7)
11 Fun and games producing exaltation (5)
12 Direction stick follows – that was Pooh's discovery (5,4)
13 Century of culture covering time, new and old (8)
15 Crawl from wood to lake (6)
18 Extremely good person held church meeting (6)
19 Offered comfort when one's cold is bad (8)
22 How casts become musical, and are daunted (4,5)
24 What's extremely chewy, sweet stuff? (5)
25 Relish money given in support (7)
26 Justify one-time scheme I concealed (7)
27 How poet might describe shady lady? (8,5)

DOWN

1 Happened by chance to see royal court (7)
2 Like freemen, reduce allegiance to monarch? (9)
3 Valuable sources in which Grimm originally found fairy-tale characters (5)
4 Troublemaker's one exemption from punishment (8)
5 Product of terrible regime? (6)
6 Engage in fight to secure some brass (4,5)
7 Putting a little money on, fascinated by horse (5)
8 Ring again to cancel (6)
14 Mow rather roughly, chopping this? (9)
16 Piece of music not paid for (9)
17 Bitter about the point coming from opposite direction (8)
18 Disparage biography omitting last year volume one should cover (6)
20 Poet's written about the old lady deserving respect (7)
21 Said peer so likely to be last in line? (6)
23 Stick man (5)
24 Shrub one may playfully cut (5)

112

ACROSS

1 Bargain on standard vegetable (7)
5 Row about stray dog (7)
9 Reason soldier's used to stop colonel retreating (5)
10 Greenness at one time surrounding church beside pub (9)
11 Militiaman stirs, ever prepared (9)
12 Old history master wanting us to be silent (5)
13 Painting of maiden by river (5)
15 Warship's run alongside one vessel in lord's possession (9)
18 Shameless farce, with a terribly wearing plot (9)
19 Observes guards (5)
21 Article in copy is early one from WI (5)
23 Non-stop flight? (9)
25 Odious traveller advanced, bagging first pair of elephants (9)
26 Spice chapter with passion (5)
27 Way pen conveys diffidence (7)
28 Particular honour (7)

DOWN

1 One escaped from Slough, another went to Kent (7)
2 Substance on butt of cigar retained by stern doctor (9)
3 Comparatively attractive name Eric changed (5)
4 Diatribe from Greek character with sauce and endless pluck (9)
5 Same number from North and South meeting in the middle, in principle (5)
6 Place for bets people put on dog, perhaps (9)
7 Like many a column, wry, with no end of humour (5)
8 Let engaging English queen come back on stage (2-5)
14 Rings to offer support, in the main (9)
16 Marker that shows opening of cave in country hill (9)
17 Conductor chosen went on bus, say (9)
18 Coarse fabric with damage raised under a dollar (7)
20 Painter, by the sound of it, superior to Constable (7)
22 Quick to knock half-formed notion (5)
23 Adversary in Troy Menelaus upset (5)
24 Destroyer abandoning last position (5)

113

ACROSS

1 As trophy, friend brought back computer (6)
5 He takes off former staff I introduced (8)
9 Conflict about note attached to van in harbour area (10)
10 One falling from tree, perhaps, that may block lane (4)
11 Confess about wine being terrible (8)
12 After short time approve material for soap (6)
13 In summit meeting leader has expert cover (4)
15 Fell for North-West Africa? (8)
18 Furiously angry about fault in legal institution (5,3)
19 One gives warning of stormy cape (4)
21 Preparation for styling hair colour son's into (6)
23 Put cover over dead caged bird (8)
25 Reversible rainwear is a fraud (4)
26 Devote energy to case studies at first (10)
27 Write to PM, having one's say, briefly (8)
28 Plate holding an iced sort of cake (6)

DOWN

2 Cause embarrassment, joining a party (5)
3 Hear about pain being imprisoned for serious crime (9)
4 Promotional material in flier (6)
5 Pub snack taken to till? (10,5)
6 Turning up to put in one's share (8)
7 Like Henry IV, accepting cape of nobleman (5)
8 Last of the light ale, perhaps? (9)
14 Meticulousness about brush used for something like scroll (9)
16 Wagner's work is long, involved with Rhine (9)
17 Feature of firearm that brings peace? (8)
20 Threaten troublemaker with death (6)
22 Apostle cutting short church malpractice (5)
24 About time to dress up for Shakespeare role (5)

114

ACROSS

1 Expression of delight as strike comes to nothing (6)
5 To a great extent, like some contracts (2,6)
9 A place in Siam, perhaps, or another Asian country (8)
10 Hit the drink (6)
11 Before I get involved in crass bloomers (8)
12 Aged? Not half – turn grey or white (6)
13 Restraining, say, royal activity (8)
15 Bank on river, see (4)
17 A small meal, say, in lots of bits (4)
19 Faithful wife writer wants to steal away (8)
20 Hate giving the lower classes an examination (6)
21 Tie up and go ashore in uncultivated area (8)
22 Left in women's accommodation in part of New York (6)
23 Destroying association of us with NI? Not I! (8)
24 Boring job done before dark, nearly – nearly, indeed (4-4)
25 Sheep sheltered by farmer in outhouse (6)

DOWN

2 A loaf each distributed – what's the problem? (8)
3 Accident on railway leading to court (8)
4 Awful bosses I have, far too fussy (9)
5 Drink it in full (7,8)
6 Positioning piano first for musical performance (7)
7 Culmination of Labour speech (8)
8 Break apart, see? (8)
14 New monies, including record coinage (9)
15 A moving performance (8)
16 Letter going astray, say, in seaside area (8)
17 British queen on ship, one from European city (8)
18 English poet in US city entering vcrsc-making contest (8)
19 Old man sitting on rear part of horse (7)

115

ACROSS

1 Here with members in order to salute (7,4)
7 Returned fish that's rotten (3)
9 Paid labourer with lots of time to wash (4,5)
10 Demand money without bill (5)
11 Bodice has bulge in the middle (7)
12 David, for example, has short time to wait (7)
13 Hand exposed as fool (5)
15 Public declaration of policy to see off famines first (9)
17 Clean hands, like Chesterton's father had (9)
19 The last thing needed in home game (5)
20 Low murmuring, funny, out of key and monotonous (7)
22 Start of instructions to look elsewhere in works for leak (7)
24 Feeling of weariness that may come from pollen nuisance (5)
25 Credit employers, taking notice of campaigners (9)
27 A possible criminal, whichever way you look at it (3)
28 Author less prolific than Ibsen? (5-6)

DOWN

1 Blind man acceptable for Bench (3)
2 Anxious to give up half-hearted West Indian music (5)
3 Sect, say, destroyed in religious frenzy (7)
4 Skilled craftsman and master builder (9)
5 Walks unsteadily in winds (5)
6 Woman from North Africa – or Western part (7)
7 Gracious act from boyfriend over recital of joke (4,5)
8 Decline to put off talk one is halfway through (11)
11 Fly over middle of the Cape? That's ungentlemanly behaviour (11)
14 In stages, new university gets notable buildings (9)
16 Calls for grape juice automatically (5,4)
18 Sort of irons used in Scottish game (7)
19 Free display out of doors (4-3)
21 Chap's excessive pride in waterproof house (5)
23 One who is acting in rep (5)
26 King is brought up to be master (3)

116

ACROSS

1 Brother's shock treatment (7)
5 Note held by unsuitable backing instruments (7)
9 Go inside and become an apprentice (5,4)
10 Help with stone for grave (5)
11 Adam's ale can give you such energy (13)
13 Copper in hard area offers a way of solving problems (8)
15 Sort of paper used for chemistry test (6)
17 Provoke former partner with a great deal, say (6)
19 Furious old bird (8)
22 Silicon, for example, counted with micros being developed (13)
25 Composer in need of tea and a pipe (5)
26 Not long before wild animals play on and around green (5,4)
27 Flame red? That won't begin to be confused with this (7)
28 Length of material, perhaps a gay red (7)

DOWN

1 Pitch that may be important factor in test (4)
2 Statute passed rapidly, set up to protect the last of British fish (7)
3 Stand erect, riding over finishing line (5)
4 One can be given out at the close of play (8)
5 What a dart could hit, pitched high? (6)
6 Perverse enjoyment of mother, split about love (9)
7 Process of change that makes death hated (7)
8 Lack of certainty as cut involves lower classes (10)
12 Attack that is crossing British line, not hard to penetrate (10)
14 To 'arm a Greek island is rash (9)
16 Deceptive investment of the Italian American in pound or yen (8)
18 Member in company I and the French put together (7)
20 One cannot individually enter this Eastern state (7)
21 See us frolicking with nude virgin (6)
23 Educator voiced disapproval over soldiers (5)
24 Festival with a lot to say (4)

117

ACROSS

1 Old club takes years restraining pusher's underhand dealing (7-6)
9 See man on board taking grain out East (9)
10 More than one spoke, possibly, identifying bones (5)
11 Government department's directions for making ditch (5)
12 Sanctimonious statement one makes for belligerent Africans (4)
13 Alliance's head heard but not quite seen (4)
15 Sound of striking entrance by king gets soldiers repeatedly running back (7)
17 Name it's given by entomologists, primarily? (7)
18 Player finding his part changed (7)
20 Poet's note received by newlyweds (7)
21 Briefly, army commander's place of detention on board (4)
22 Employer getting rid of doorkeeper's husband (4)
23 Get rid of animal of inferior breeding (5)
26 Return unknown, initially, in old age (5)
27 It's mixed up with a man or a woman in love (9)
28 Inform about churchman and peer's bitter altercation (8,5)

DOWN

1 Combination of ageism, sexism, and nepotism? (4,3,3,4)
2 Delightful people, as seen in good French art (5)
3 Self-absorbed fellow covers fare with small coin (10)
4 Strange story about king and one supporter of royal family (7)
5 Head back with bovine animal, say? One upset ram (7)
6 Colour of apple crumble (4)
7 Shouting about social upheaval? It's heard in the mountains (9)
8 Query about Saturday or Sunday, say, for satanic ritual? (7,7)
14 Mental aberration bishop linked with severe weather (10)
16 Slow progress of woman held up by sailor on ship (9)
19 Stressful way of carrying out examination (7)
20 Pub drink taken outside a good deal (7)
24 Severely criticise cook before fire (5)
25 Fancy assistant moving article from top to bottom! (4)

118

ACROSS

1 Where hammer falls promptly (2,3,4)
6 To catch girl, ring is needed (5)
9 Fine point producing blow-out (5)
10 Fish around to catch by hand – that's said to be "hands-on" (9)
11 Pierrot undaunted, to some extent, in impressive hall (7)
12 Dictionary I study in pursuit of old word for "law" (7)
13 A cold part of London – not a leg to be seen – just part of one (8,6)
17 Of course declarer's upset about this much older partner (6-8)
21 Speeds between points in darkness (7)
23 Dog seen to bare teeth without backing off (7)
25 In agreement with letter? Not I, for one (9)
26 As form of punishment, king has knight dismissed (5)
27 No way in – that's bad (5)
28 Not 10 to three, roughly one to 100 (9)

DOWN

1 Away on holiday, achieved delivery (3-5)
2 Food and drink (5)
3 Caught up in net, dangle, squirming (9)
4 Satisfy animal, stuffing it with vegetables (7)
5 Bill, a mischievous creature, climbing into water channel (7)
6 Milky fluid from past times (5)
7 After wine, clergymen used to show penitence (9)
8 Pupil no longer has desire for geometric construction (6)
14 Rain's held off – bad luck! (4,5)
15 One carping, having a pound, keeping it quiet (3-6)
16 Distracted if centre is out of position (8)
18 Pleasingly simple lament cut short by worker (7)
19 Close match, in which one retires (7)
20 Warning signal – has to be a trick (6)
22 Professional co-ordinates authorisation for agent (5)
24 Runs into vessel's bow (5)

119

Warning! This puzzle was designed for a particular date, and contains a few less familiar solutions

ACROSS

1   Note – this is about to tease people (5)
4   Go underground, unable to settle down (5-4)
9   In other words, editor finalises sharper version (9)
10 Disgust dissenter, having change of heart (5)
11 Firm beset by a French delay oddly showing no anxiety (13)
14 Last act of *Endgame*, coming very soon for 23 (4)
15 In real trouble, having to swallow bread and cheese (10)
18 23 given less than hour, coming in late (10)
19 A small case of being quite silly, no question (4)
21 28 and 23 meet to see *The French Connection* (7,6)
24 Bird, in practice, following duck to lake (5)
25 See source of cackling and smile – *A Knight at the Opera* (9)
27 Plan to surprise carol singers, after extra rest (3,2,4)
28 Final translation of 21 – first of it appearing today (5)

DOWN

1   Inquisitor turning force on first man brought up (10)
2   One mischievous and playful, primarily (3)
3   23's task in *Mission Impossible*? (6)
4   Someone from over the border in Scotland (9)
5   Staff joined by popular French master (5)
6   Wonderful place to live, but on shaky foundations for 23 (8)
7   Role of Othello reviewed by proxy as a hit (11)
8   Top award – falsely glittering for 23 (4)
12 Clever, keeping in also previous PC facility (3,3,5)
13 Bill has grasped nothing, climbing into danger with slopes all around (10)
16 Restrictions put on latest type of ammunition (5,4)
17 Some hate filling boxes with text (8)
20 Served up a popular lunch, perhaps fillet (6)
22 Cold dish incomplete – put in second spicy sauce (5)
23 Cod – the fish provided by 21 (4)
26 Play the game, finally wiser! (1,1,1)

ACROSS

1 Gave satisfactory all-round performance as point-to-pointer? (5,3,7)
9 Say bad things about a dire gent, possibly (9)
10 Like black stuff in dock (5)
11 Futility of opposing it in any case (6)
12 Protection against cats and dogs (8)
13 Pub – English place where things happen (6)
15 Produce good sketches of water source (4-4)
18 What you may find up your tree – an ape, originally? (8)
19 Philosopher on the street who's reluctant to leave? (6)
21 Question and answer sequence in verse (8)
23 Like number system replacing abaci? That's about right (6)
26 Warlike people in city area one repulsed (5)
27 Conniving old emperor jeers (2,7)
28 Dinner's produced with such lack of enthusiasm for diner (4-11)

DOWN

1 Where patient may be confined with foul plague (7)
2 Harmless gas that gets nobody cross, upset (5)
3 Drug jab – Capone is after it (9)
4 Excitement in race (4)
5 Transformed my career in agricultural business (8)
6 Important little woman inhabiting ruin (5)
7 Male in army becoming sucker for the bigger guns (9)
8 Piece of canvas or shot silk, say (7)
14 Bird a duck, we hear? A parrot, actually (9)
16 A line of terrain with flowers either side is a landmark (9)
17 A fish heading north, skirting small island (8)
18 PM a person of little significance? That's hard (7)
20 Gives new part to versatile actress (7)
22 Austrian psychologist in German state (5)
24 Black mud in port, for example (5)
25 Singing without words? Get away! (4)

ACROSS

1 It gives the audience confidence in the theatre (5,7)
9 Carpenter's requirements on hand (5)
10 One's able to negotiate new terms (9)
11 Make a bigger ruff from an obvious remnant (9)
12 Use the house phone briefly in this establishment (5)
13 Opera's iron maiden (6)
15 Daring fraud in a resort (8)
18 Subsidise country mansion in inferior position (4,4)
19 Eating out, have a piece of cake (6)
22 A miner, say, gets medal (5)
24 Postpone vehicle deliveries on railway (5,4)
26 Now and then expressed admiration for this paper (9)
27 Dreadful feeling concealed by gangster (5)
28 Men's formal wear – for funerals, say? (7,5)

DOWN

1 Impose punishment that makes offender see red (4,3)
2 Live bear (5)
3 One way to buy *Hard Times*? On the contrary (4,5)
4 Suspend riding – it's becoming an obsession (4-2)
5 Betraying what's in the bag, perhaps (8)
6 Manage to raise horse – it takes an age (5)
7 Seize property from girl's school (8)
8 Unemotional time in firm (6)
14 Speaks passionately about church in dismal confusion (8)
16 Fly off and put in appearance in magic place (9)
17 Woman's lover has to reckon with crew (5,3)
18 Loud and blaring club (6)
20 Out of the top drawer, packing cases for junior churchmen (7)
21 Can present pair with a single child (6)
23 One without drink spotted in party – same again? (5)
25 Doubtful start to vacation with shivering fit (5)

ACROSS

1 The CID puts false manufactured evidence about (8,2)
7 This insect may be noisy now, however (4)
9 People keep score without writing anything down (8)
10 Mean mate shot (6)
11 Momentous communication (6)
12 Take notice of number badly beaten (4,4)
13 Hang on to burden, say (4)
15 Sociable fellow, not very different (10)
18 Monster fowl getting at cereal (10)
20 Gallery ultimately displaying no old masters (4)
21 Point to man who works for sheriff? (8)
24 From mathematicians we required a solution (6)
26 A way to move without exertion (6)
27 Make a careless mistake, and you finally get beaten – with knobs on (8)
28 Take a quick look and observe turning (4)
29 Flames disturbed dons by fire (10)

DOWN

2 At home, kid composed operetta (3,6)
3 Primordial god, one ignored by painter (5)
4 Henry running away in the gloom (4-5)
5 Senior member, the oldest poet around (7)
6 Goody-goody finally got the bird (5)
7 Our group will be in good state of health (4-5)
8 Name applied to father's femme fatale (5)
14 Evaluate and purchase shares (4,5)
16 A tragic lover keeping kiss for great general (9)
17 Without clothing – nude, possibly (9)
19 Fashionable and extravagant childhood (7)
22 Man, say, importing last of coconut fibre (5)
23 Stevenson, not a bachelor without restraint (2,3)
25 Manage to retain ointment (5)

123

ACROSS

1 Use coin side to make this, perhaps (8)
5 Fight shy of champ, two points ahead (6)
10 One chooses to allow each player to take part (7,8)
11 Fish hard to pack into old-fashioned cask (7)
12 Scientist turned criminal by one Pope? (7)
13 Dishes that can be heated anew and overcooked (8)
15 Furry creature with shrill bark, right? (5)
18 They help one see the details of what's required (5)
20 Sailors leading us into place of punishment (8)
23 King heading East to recover after setback (7)
25 American flier's unhappy letter (4,3)
26 No new statement by a novice driver lacking training (3-12)
27 English horse last in Epsom Derby, for instance (6)
28 Inexperienced and prosaic? (8)

DOWN

1 Notes how long Paris was involved in war (6)
2 How De Gaulle announced his resignation? (4,2,3)
3 Saint on the side of breaking evil (7)
4 Tongue, for example, describable as "mouthpiece" (5)
6 Poet with tough exterior, from what we hear (7)
7 Inn has nothing in the rum line (5)
8 Engage in fighting wizards (8)
9 Making learner take part in play (4,4)
14 Fade out broadcast after a dreadful final sentence (4-2-2)
16 Steps taken to commemorate naval commander (4,5)
17 Antagonise sergeant with new order (8)
19 Parking carriage outside plant (7)
21 Maligning a vehicle I have (7)
22 Contemplated learner I kept in – what comes over pupil? (6)
24 Antelope – beat it! (5)
25 Ship's officer given more pay after switch of partners (5)

124

ACROSS

1 Slam nobody else can make (4-9)
8 Copies some of the main points on a page (4)
9 Singer not getting on with instrument wedding guest heard (5)
10 Hide in moorland (4)
11 Sort of road that can damage a trailer (8)
12 Fast that is moved for a festival (6)
13 Party policies needed to get people on board (10)
16 Bird that's quickly dropped in America (4)
17 Doctor leaves Arctic region, taking fish (4)
18 Wearisome place old actors went to, for a change (6,4)
20 Stock title (6)
22 Model exhibitions are staged here (8)
24 Face being placed in retirement (4)
25 Fascinated by runs included in start of jazz piece (5)
26 Bird unable to fly has time to ditch (4)
27 Having paint in mind, like artists? (13)

DOWN

1 A student of the occult? Darwin was (15)
2 Strong line taken in pedestrianised border town? (5)
3 It takes time with a twisted leg to find a carriage (9)
4 Nearly all abuse fashionable hormone (7)
5 You won't be out of pocket after this accident (2-3)
6 One may be in a silly position to take chances (9)
7 Drink offered by Soviet statesman having inflammatory impact (7,8)
14 Comprehensive sporting triumph in which one never loses the lead (5,4)
15 Complaint of the hot-headed (9)
19 Cheese with a portion of apricot tart (7)
21 Pick flower of a certain type (5)
23 Own daughter embraced by a short child (5)

125

ACROSS

1 Woman joined by father and son in the plains (6)
5 Soft wood from vessel identified in record (8)
9 Popular author providing the finest wines, we hear? (4-6)
10 Deliver balls for sports stadium in US (4)
11 Obsession with gold in lake belonging to 12 (8)
12 Sort of car one was willing to leave (6)
13 Stone work almost completely assembled (4)
15 Obsessive manoeuvring in court judge finally accepted (8)
18 Official order prematurely closed mine that's worn out (8)
19 Trail of wild animal? Lion, for example (4)
21 Couples beginning muffins especially like this breakfast food (6)
23 Mature relationship to nature, for example, seen in poet's work (3-5)
25 The factory whose run is mediocre? (4)
26 Like something in the kitchen involved with several parties (10)
27 About to run – had to seek help (8)
28 Religious belief exists in those opposed to US (6)

DOWN

2 Stories about soldiers in field of conflict (5)
3 Work for one's living (9)
4 Money that is used to support commercial venture (6)
5 Where sleepers are found at every point (3,5,3,4)
6 Party Figaro cut short, given signal (8)
7 It's up to British soldiers to build this automated machine (5)
8 Inadvertent humour in Cockney's pursuit of game (9)
14 Premature opinion written with pride (9)
16 Hops in here to get ready for a drink (4-5)
17 Athlete's son – one making an impression (8)
20 Singularly trifling sum for an oil producer (6)
22 Thus a meal ticket received an enthusiastic reaction (5)
24 Agency's resources (5)

ACROSS

1 Employment situation's hard in Midlands town (8)
5 State investing nothing in fourth scheme (6)
9 Modern craft that has its place in Paris (8)
10 Maintain a fine business (6)
12 English duet composed after French piece of music (5)
13 Moth wife found in open area in forest (9)
14 Professional from university town checking text (5-7)
18 New metal goal constructed for annual school match (4,4,4)
21 Minor fictional public school? Not quite (4,5)
23 Computer equipment doctor's given by practice (5)
24 Casual piece of work producing strange book (3,3)
25 Refer to one of the gospels, perhaps, about one result of division (8)
26 Dirty-looking husband on board pleasure boat (6)
27 Expertly clothing woman in charming fashion (8)

DOWN

1 Gate that always has a keeper (6)
2 Call for record (4,2)
3 With this result, crowds are content, possibly (5,4)
4 Group loyalty revealed by link with 15 (3,6,3)
6 Volunteer not available to serve king (5)
7 From the start of Romans (2,6)
8 Lower classes very eager to be included in my political agitation (8)
11 Ride drunk needs to avoid (5-2-5)
15 Mother contributed to change in university once (4,5)
16 Potter joining one club after another, endlessly (8)
17 Ask one fellow who's the main deity? (8)
19 By splitting membership fee, it becomes excellent (6)
20 Jolly way to introduce church meeting (6)
22 Take back most of the idle talk (5)

ACROSS

1 Adore eating a good salad plant (6)
5 Fielder really wants to excel (8)
9 One boy on pier docked junk (8)
10 Quarrel during Indian meal (6)
11 The bird's a ruddy duck (8)
12 One in difficult position, with oxygen cut (6)
13 Take age about eating one slab of chocolate (8)
15 Right way for King Arthur to call his seneschal? (4)
17 Relax, receiving money in rent (4)
19 To show approval, then reject some, is humbug (8)
20 Register monarch's wave (6)
21 Wheat, perhaps, for making bread (4,4)
22 Fastidious duke isn't unknown (6)
23 Atrocious crime soldiers committed in hatred (8)
24 Very precise arrangement of ours captivating musical prince (8)
25 Old tribesman died first, having to hang (6)

DOWN

2 Fail to notice finished appearance (8)
3 Element hating wealth? That's not English (8)
4 Sees Latin translation key (9)
5 To get rich, do job for tailor? (4,4,7)
6 Expression of distaste, but I'm in favour (7)
7 Over-stout and weak, getting back support (8)
8 Precisely locate cask with some beer – empty? (8)
14 Run into the second keep's entrance (9)
15 Mounted guard, free to put in a shot (8)
16 A policeman initially working steadily, being in force (8)
17 As detailed description, mine's bad example (8)
18 Swallowing tons, debauched, like Dionysus (8)
19 City street covered by hail (7)

ACROSS

1 More than one place for a meeting (4)
3 American bounder and knave do a lot of talking (10)
9 A medic rejected the last piece of music (4)
10 Wife getting drunk outside and excessively stoned? (10)
12 Author of religious type, we hear (9)
13 Entertainment to put in for the rest of the Japanese (5)
14 Bright colour of wine served with chicken (6,6)
18 Traditionally, the object of kiss and tell? (7,5)
21 Opposed to gang-leader getting on (5)
22 Put together grandiose construction (9)
24 Dessert that keeps naughty children initially silent (10)
25 Place in Scotland where anything goes? (4)
26 First-class fare too good for the workers (5,5)
27 Non-medical name for split personality (4)

DOWN

1 Brave Rugby forwards going for beauty treatment (4,4)
2 How his followers viewed Lenin, say, as a star (3,5)
4 Forging equipment hidden by Russian villagers (5)
5 Irish breed found in County Down (5,4)
6 In fact, one's gone astray in test of maturity, legally (3,2,7)
7 Having got inside, stole capital (6)
8 Powerful men getting cramps, say (6)
11 A curious sort, rational about interpretation of signs (12)
15 Measure of beer in long glass (4,2,3)
16 Spoils by reform, perhaps (8)
17 Entertainment with drink provided on trip (3,5)
19 Administer shock treatment (6)
20 Front of newspaper covering naughty robbery (6)
23 Author adding final line to a couple of essays (5)

ACROSS

1 Exactly where does the rent go? (2,3,6)
7 Little fairy endlessly flitted around (3)
9 Concern about technique needed for ornamental drawing (9)
10 More pleasant French resort by river (5)
11 Right across road you'll find petrol (7)
12 Holds up kangaroo mother – finally managed to find pouch (7)
13 Crop I planted in the middle of lots of paths (5)
15 Standard group of workers employed by plant (5,4)
17 Contemporary code broken by strange misbehaviour (9)
19 Inside part of French bathroom fitting (5)
20 Soup I left, making mouth sore (7)
22 Gods largely ill-disposed (7)
24 Inclined to join a fight (5)
25 Showing extreme desire to join Labour association (9)
27 Island of vital importance (3)
28 Keep quiet in case operation is very fast with only brief pauses (7-4)

DOWN

1 Twitch at regular intervals? (3)
2 Constellation reportedly in the shape of a doughnut (5)
3 Being responsible for love I have found wearing (7)
4 Former wife gets most of premier residence and personal funds (9)
5 Bill dropped by player, a lock (5)
6 Weakened by ill-health, fell (3,4)
7 Bound to catch corrupt cleric with no way out (9)
8 "Waged war like Galahad" reported magazine (11)
11 One must pull strings to operate this firework (7,4)
14 Secure against loss if my dinner not completely cooked (9)
16 Johnny-come-lately, one given one award after another (9)
18 Take heed, around zero Celsius, climbing and turning on ice (7)
19 Wear something to cover face up with insect around (7)
21 Some national assistance used for drink (5)
23 Be discriminatory – cut off first son (5)
26 Doctor taking a break (3)

130

ACROSS

1 Notice lake surrounded by ranges in barren area (8)
6 Point to fish making smell (6)
9 Already tumulus incorporates inner chamber (6)
10 Umbrella making for warm and dry top (3,5)
11 Block stopping light for shade (5,3)
12 I succeeded former Eastern queen (6)
13 Destiny Hindu god takes right to heart (5)
14 Alert, performing the dance (2,3,4)
17 Flustered, I locate BR carriage (9)
19 Dear Virginia vanishes in avoidance of publicity (5)
22 Not much left in view (6)
23 World exhibition – certainly it will be on film (8)
24 He can't render lead as good as gold (8)
25 Island explorer (6)
26 Ready to display picture of Dickens (6)
27 Greeting descendant of Noah in national park (8)

DOWN

2 Beheaded first woman king caught in European state (7)
3 It's terribly clear to me one will miss deadline (9)
4 Become better educated, say? Never again (2,4)
5 Two chaps before wedding, perhaps, behave very formally (5,2,8)
6 Skill shown up, in a sense, in last part of race (8)
7 Literary work Fitzgerald produced after a month (7)
8 Fooling around in drug operation (9)
13 First impulse of immoral woman going after thrills (4-5)
15 Play for country (9)
16 First words of Hamlet's speech garbled to queen – it's drink (4,4)
18 Composer gripped to pen start of Requiem (7)
20 Contemptible person put on charge in force (7)
21 Electrician installing link termination in boxes (6)

131

Across

1 Bird settled by musician buying instrument? (8)
6 One may be downtrodden in Oxford (6)
9 Broadcast live beside a large inland sea (6)
10 Suitable with nothing for a change? Just the reverse (8)
11 Unconditional claim not allowed at first (8)
12 Band beginning to sail East on tour (6)
13 Pass in reading, writing, or arithmetic set by a head (5)
14 Man and woman recently signed up for union (9)
17 Coarse material for the royals (9)
19 Supports a man fellows heard about (5)
22 Greatest sum to free before closing of account (6)
23 Working classes featured in one show or another (8)
24 Superfluous ornament underneath coat, originally (8)
25 In Turkey, mount paintings a painter dropped in (6)
26 Female adviser rejected passion in mature years (6)
27 Port's okay, oddly, when eating old meat (8)

Down

2 Tax excessively – that's how our government rules English (7)
3 Crossword clues are in order like this (9)
4 Daughter employed in so-called architect's plant (6)
5 Deliberately ignore appearance in alternative fashion (4,3,5,3)
6 Mischievously intimate about his misbehaving (8)
7 Mineral oil freely distributed over plant (7)
8 Refreshments found in team's quarters (9)
13 Cabinet-maker's new deal (9)
15 Gloss over a series of defeats (9)
16 Charge a large number entering vessels together (8)
18 I am going to pond to catch a second duck (7)
20 Achieve redemption as a sort of miracle (7)
21 Greeting sailor involved in act of piracy (6)

ACROSS

1   It'll be done at some stage, to furnish new flats (5-8)
8   European has to work very hard to finish early (4)
9   Temperate stretch of coast, about fifty miles (5)
10 A piece of cake – take it thus to avoid stress (4)
11 Govt. Department's power covers Eastern cross-country route (5,3)
12 I love you   originally smitten somewhere in Somerset (6)
13 Struggle with Bill's opinions (10)
16 Thrill given to 18, for a start (4)
17 Returned half of original payment by cheque (4)
18 One getting well oiled before joining TT set? (10)
20 Son's quick finding fault (6)
22 Turn up twice? Are you serious? (4,4)
24 Test new version, or retain original one (4)
25 Delivered cards, with a last letter from Greece (5)
26 One can sort of turn back (4)
27 Regular fluctuation in frequency of arrivals and departures (7,6)

DOWN

1   Blocking everyone else's view (4-11)
2   Pop legend lives? That's crazy! (5)
3   Chance for movement from new bowler – two ducks and maiden follow (5,4)
4   Can holy order set out to be happy and calm? (7)
5   Knowing past planetary investigation (3-2)
6   Game to exploit a freeze, taking stick for one's goals (3,6)
7   I'll produce copy detailing society's activities (6,9)
14 Set I bear with turned up to party (5,2,2)
15 Three-quarters of the team back me up in union contest (5-4)
19 Thanks new clerk as one prepared to take on tasks? (7)
21 Highly effective form of vocal communication (5)
23 Channel to do some filming for audience (5)

133

ACROSS

1 Careless initial omission from logical statement (6)
4 Better to keep cupboard locked with this sort of key? (8)
10 Son involved with Etonians in scandal (9)
11 Bowled unfairly from one end to the other, we hear (5)
12 Ship's officer holding church service at last in cutter (7)
13 Attacked, taking bishop? Invalid position (4-3)
14 Soldier leading military unit is firm, allowing the general no say (7,7)
19 Said to conceal explorer with difficulty in part of capital (4,4,6)
21 Fight using old missile (7)
24 A bishop pursued by extra devil (7)
26 Board about to advance money to the writer (5)
27 On Oxford course, each learner gives impression of royal authority (5,4)
28 Not one old man has appeal to a European girl (8)
29 Form of insect in new strain (6)

DOWN

1 Pick up account of American's career (6)
2 One I no longer need to doctor given cosmetic treatment (9)
3 Criticise nominees for office in America (5)
5 Two books taken from college (5)
6 Not one of the original party constructing Camelot with king (9)
7 Chuck wicket away, bowled, and get beat (5)
8 At present we have no means to keep a daughter (8)
9 Excellent source for pitch on which to have sport (4-4)
15 Air proves bad – this may ease breathing (9)
16 Flower's regular sequence, opening about a minute before noon (8)
17 Notice time, with people twice interrupting to make correction (9)
18 Applause about question in house taken by Prime Minister (8)
20 A bite makes one reel (6)
22 Clerical vestment seen on an English martyr (5)
23 Lead away from stairs, being giddy (5)
25 A new style for Bruckner, say (5)

134

Across

1 Foot of legendary bird in the East (7)
5 No native set out on crime (7)
9 Doctor bound to admit tax is not without reason (9)
10 Represents agency (5)
11 Bestial murder represented in play (6,7)
13 Statements to the press not allowed in Israel (4-4)
15 Wretched harvest not begun, so go hungry (6)
17 Useless king becoming more conceited (6)
19 Native servant (8)
22 It controls the right of way – should suit Channel trippers (5,8)
25 The most remarkable of siege-works in Ancient Greece? (5)
26 With stronghold captured in advance, Duke cheered up (9)
27 George (the First) not so fat, one gathers (7)
28 Agreed to accommodate desire of leading lady (7)

Down

1 Worker who can't stick the heat, in short (4)
2 Cycle inventor chap supplied with padded seat (7)
3 Allergic reaction in the colonies (5)
4 Request to take one's food among the competitors (8)
5 A serious trouble spot raised in conference (6)
6 Body appointed to pledge support for ball (9)
7 Snake – find a couple for a Cockney chap (7)
8 Greece runs revolutionary revival (10)
12 Shifting lots of drink out of mean dwelling (10)
14 Load never adjusted – this, as result? (9)
16 Ate fish special menu's included (8)
18 Fashionable sin holds nothing for Bill (7)
20 Reduce freedom of strong man, we hear (7)
21 Shopkeeper's more outrageous in conversation (6)
23 Key part of Jumbo (5)
24 Slack in line taken up by fish (4)

135

ACROSS

1 Excellent rent, highly profitable (3-7)
6 Help a Yankee, perhaps (4)
9 Community restricting a German serf's status (10)
10 Social group, sound as a bell, but no good (4)
12 Check price on port in Spain and provide new refreshment (12)
15 Emotionally identify English politician, at his office at last (9)
17 Girl mostly comprehends old Polynesian language (5)
18 Part of intestine or pelvic bone, say (5)
19 Favourite weapon to contain union leader's peevishness (9)
20 Name home in a French document? It's not settled (12)
24 Immoral conduct of counsel disposing of notice (4)
25 Baker found former transport firm satisfactory (10)
26 Baby food king's son consumed in this state (4)
27 English article actually written in airy way (10)

DOWN

1 Wander to other side of river going north (4)
2 Run fast and hide (4)
3 Expect too much of single male in laird's position (12)
4 Arrive with expedition and get arrested (3,2)
5 Careless fellow with broken leg in Northern Ireland (9)
7 Foreign beauty's source of drug (10)
8 Was apt to go round upward slope, being less tough (10)
11 It preserves notes penned by starchy alter ego (12)
13 Brief note makes house tremble (10)
14 Lists of supplementary material and piano pieces, perhaps (10)
16 Bring in a set of books of great significance (9)
21 Man, for example, securing employment ultimately as rope-maker? (5)
22 Way in which lake adjoins bay (4)
23 It's still all right without an affirmative vote (4)

ACROSS

1 All but one of the party stand to lose their seats at this (7,6)
8 Man and woman getting married (4)
9 Unconscious king, shot by an archer (5)
10 Become a business executive (4)
11 Siren making everyone jump (3-5)
12 Short book about a Caribbean republic (6)
13 Policeman admitting bizarre old laws might be nonsense (10)
16 Snacks as enjoyable as tasty savoury starters (4)
17 Long letter wanting short answer (4)
18 Oversleep, say, and be late for public appearance (3,2,5)
20 Millions one lost in withdrawing capital account (6)
22 Figure female's about to improve (8)
24 Establish a record (4)
25 Writer making money out East with one book (5)
26 Man of the right moving to the left (4)
27 As China might be, collectively, when in a mess (6,7)

DOWN

1 Moderate idea H. Ford reworked with Model T (6-2-3-4)
2 Problem on account of tree (5)
3 About to fail with bid? Almost a disaster (5,4)
4 Accurate volume written by American with a novel ending (7)
5 King in Bible said to have great memory (5)
6 Fresh out of, initially, vermouth on the rocks (9)
7 In the main, don't offer resistance (4,4,3,4)
14 Solemn old characters defending church (9)
15 Fellow who's retired hurt is new opener (9)
19 Port where Hesperus wrecked? Not right (7)
21 Rebel without a cause (5)
23 Language rich in dialects, if you look into it (5)

ACROSS

1   Evaluate young reporter that's returned coarse material (7)
5   A woman's got round soldiers before now (7)
9   Extended picnic? (9)
10 Greedily devour Cheddar, perhaps (5)
11 Speed of light measurement by old instrument (5)
12 Deficient agency secretary's skill (9)
13 Resolve to discourage race on motorway (13)
17 A cousin's confused about Greek pi (13)
21 Essential final triplets in quaint Couperin music (9)
24 Boredom is universal during middle of Wimbledon game (5)
25 Do this after start to alarm and confuse (5)
26 Soothing girl encountered in hospital department (9)
27 Meeting person endlessly behind on tax (7)
28 Drink to soldiers highest in rank (7)

DOWN

1   Baroque composer penning right old boring bit (6)
2   Taken up the garden path following bed with unknown succulent (9)
3   Popular music's opening harmony (7)
4   Disturbed marmoset left in a state of confusion (9)
5   Gold finish coming off designer sound-system (5)
6   Series of rows upset *Great Expectations'* central characters (7)
7   Unfinished road being up leads to tailback along major artery (5)
8   Nigel's involved with DIY rendering (8)
14 Harmless and popular old copper kept in mind (9)
15 Hypocritical to take part in sin, since religious (9)
16 Revolutionary partisan showing ambition (8)
18 Make scores of sixty, say (7)
19 As one does on the tiles, drink too much? (7)
20 Six rupees a day? Goodness! (6)
22 Newspaper that folded when this one came out (5)
23 Thin novel getting royalty (5)

137

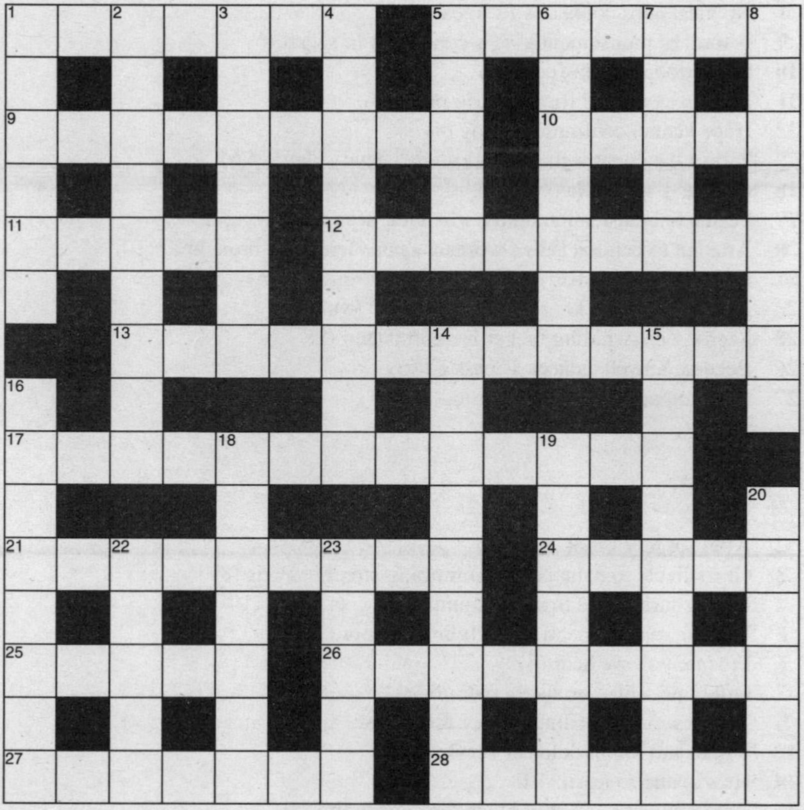

ACROSS

1 No meal cubs cooked is fit to eat (10)
9 A form of punishment king's concealed in secret (6)
10 Some troops are in flight (8)
11 Huge area needed for climbing plant (8)
12 Hope kennel confines this dog (4)
13 Part of the country that's against alc? That's daft! (4,6)
15 Forbear's burden (7)
17 Seems to be listening avidly when learners turn very quiet (7)
20 Attempt to convert fallen woman – pure female is brought in (10)
21 Hardy heroine in fix, rejected by spouse initially (4)
23 Pressure with backlog resulting in jam? (8)
25 Secret society hiding racket back in island (8)
26 Become unwell as neck is twisted (6)
27 Cleaning up, that is, and settling score (10)

DOWN

2 After surgery I took drug (6)
3 One's liable to damage shoe climbing street in Paris (8)
4 Flower-girl whose Spanish counterpart gets drunk (10)
5 Mistake, planting elm stupidly in bad spot (7)
6 Procure pot, we hear (4)
7 Order me a lilac or another shrub (8)
8 Tar uses mat, shuffling part of foot (10)
12 Some land job in delivery service (6,4)
14 He's bound to learn (10)
16 Song and dance created by soldier under fire (8)
18 Attractive way to finish off making 14 (8)
19 Clerical cover-up at the highest level? (7)
22 Run unfinished, having collected a form of injury (6)
24 Oversees functions (4)

139

ACROSS

1 Criterion magistrates have to observe (9)
6 Loud organ let fly (5)
9 Missing diva's opening, singer has to begin again (7)
10 Girl about 50 beyond limit comes to a sort of stop (7)
11 The recurrent Fall of Man, say (5)
12 Players a team has to discard (4,5)
14 Girl with plenty of dates (3)
15 Telephone to authorise instruction to start meeting (4,2,5)
17 Plant that's least restrained and widespread (11)
19 In a sorry state, having failed to rise (3)
20 Magistrate's given a time to execute key cut-throat (3-3-3)
22 Woman employed to clean (5)
24 A major worry for David's wife (7)
26 Sort of reception in which you may have to stand (7)
27 Butcher not starting to provide fish (5)
28 Beset by time scramble, news channels become most pressing (9)

DOWN

1 Beefy nobleman? (5)
2 Curious about mature climbing flowers (7)
3 Listen to male cat held up in anguish (9)
4 Enunciated clearly, being well-connected? (11)
5 Sort of beer available in King's Head, say (3)
6 Miss Poste's plants (5)
7 Intrude somehow without being heard (7)
8 Plant, or birch (9)
13 Protest about time taken to clean up the lounge (7-4)
14 Sensational performance setting off dome alarm (9)
16 To discard, one throws this on the table (9)
18 Unfinished at the time of departure (7)
19 This sort of verse isn't free, in the main (7)
21 Visibly prepared to eat feast (5)
23 Sort of meat found in chop (5)
25 Wreath that's left over (3)

ACROSS

1 Unscrupulous heroine's signal to unknown swindler (5,5)
6 Confer about male kitchen worker (4)
9 I make a mistake about Mediterranean area – it's not important (10)
10 Moderate affluence (4)
12 Momentous news about pound flourishing (5-7)
15 Bow to receive honour as nice change (9)
17 Cast metal mounted with parts reversed (5)
18 It's safe to signal (5)
19 Swelling the crowd (9)
20 Only one spade left, perhaps, for emptying graves (3,4,5)
24 Ruth, a young girl in America (4)
25 1000 I bet, but with "0" omitted in error (10)
26 Move against current leader of religious movement (4)
27 This could be put out to dry the road (10)

DOWN

1 Across the river, large vessel (4)
2 Eccentric vehicle departs (4)
3 Give voice to cry of pain and run, showing cowardice (6,6)
4 Tool like a spade – but no spades in this shed (5)
5 Coming to life again, more sensible over money (9)
7 Sound amplifier needed by some judging endless Verdi opera (7,3)
8 French crew, on time, transported goods (10)
11 A skilled craftsman, the PM (7-5)
13 Welcoming a bishop, let loose (10)
14 Pamper in comfortable place for retirement (down under) (10)
16 Unusual in-flight entertainment's beginning – entertainment after dark (9)
21 Verminous and irritable (5)
22 One has a place in sun – I think (4)
23 Textile worker's dreadful report (4)

ACROSS

1   Under time pressure, revised kitchen catalogs (7,3,5)
9   Water from an embankment given to farm animals (5,4)
10 Spike with broken point (5)
11 Deny broadcast's drowned by distracting noise (6)
12 Exotic bird puts a libertine in a temper (8)
13 Seasoning from stone container put back (6)
15 This connects me with various crimes – how fascinating! (8)
18 Deliver cargo of sponge (8)
19 Piano, say, used in club (6)
21 Track made by dragoon (8)
23 Medical book written in smoother ballpoint (6)
26 Military commander's home once more (5)
27 Dissident exhorted to change and accept love (9)
28 Expansion of corporation in historical period quietly studied (6-3,6)

DOWN

1   11 in a group of musicians in performance (7)
2   Collect incorporated in a church service (5)
3   Part of plane – whole seen to be damaged (4,5)
4   End of story, as the saying goes (4)
5   Man upset the second time in fear sounded like an ass (8)
6   Drink up, Dad, before it gets cold (5)
7   During Thursday, English revolutionary is busy (2,3,4)
8   Relations call up in connection with motion (7)
14 Head girl team-leader was informed about (3,6)
16 Play as alternative to *Cats*? (9)
17 Save articles in soft fabric (8)
18 Military equipment company receives attention (7)
20 Lessened – cut by about 50 (7)
22 Put in actual name of an organ (5)
24 Distinguishing mark of tailless nocturnal creature (5)
25 Ultimately this might uglify eye (4)

142

ACROSS

1 Fishing adviser said cat must go back – it takes fish (9)
6 Fruit pulp – oh, no! (5)
9 Tear off to secure *Times* special edition (5)
10 Collection available after fall, not in spring (9)
11 Hull's the target for this missile (7)
12 State school, one with a place for son inside (7)
13 Men locked together in conflict (9,2,3)
17 Constitutional reform leaving many questions unanswered (5,9)
21 What traveller carries in toboggan is a joke (7)
23 Holding degree, I understand a Japanese art form (7)
25 Complicated art repels mural craftsman (9)
26 Clung to by climber, I struggled (5)
27 Forcing oneself forward to back up throw (5)
28 Mob leader expected to accept point put by giant (9)

DOWN

1 Cousin of ours sending fruit round to consume (5,3)
2 Italian footballers start off season (5)
3 Ignores evidence of spring (6,3)
4 Ruin depressed English playwright (7)
5 Muscle from dinosaur missing middle section (7)
6 Singer is favourite around ladies' organisation (5)
7 King penguin originally fed outside old shelter (9)
8 Used to be inexperienced, raising capital (6)
14 It can clarify how vocalist introduces himself to girl? (9)
15 Spike becoming heartless and showing impatience (9)
16 One Creakle caned often having to lift bottom right up and spread legs apart (8)
18 Protested scripture was not infallible (7)
19 Wit from English, stock examples (7)
20 For such a good meal, drink outside and drink inside (4-2)
22 Fittingly put to use after change of heart (5)
24 Getting on, making name in a band performance (5)

143

ACROSS

1 Commotion made by drunk, mostly, crossing border (9)
6 Subject getting to elect no king (5)
9 Modified training received by female journalist (7)
10 Conductor in English tram's unusually old (7)
11 House left by German king (5)
12 Collected writings presenting a new religious doctrine out East (9)
13 Religious type from Yale straying in all directions (8)
15 Roguish principal in combinations (4)
19 Attack lecher (4)
20 It's dodgy on stormy ocean for one (8)
23 Collection taken by party official is complete (4-5)
24 Witty remark one let drop in this vessel (5)
26 Getting away from noise, returned outside? (7)
27 Flower to be got from girlfriend (7)
28 Docked gently, using this sort of anchor (5)
29 Touchy person can fight about article in German (9)

DOWN

1 Rascal's humorous retort about Conservative wit (9)
2 Make into law, upsetting an Eastern court (5)
3 In old-fashioned style, dismissed fourth form? (8)
4 Appearing in belt, like 19, for example (8)
5 Time to show such antagonism? (6)
6 Quake producing extremes of terror over capital (6)
7 Spicy sort of literary miscellany? (3-6)
8 Friend's exclamation immediately after entering (5)
14 Was ordered by unknown individual to settle in African country (9)
16 Exhorted converts to accept nothing schismatic (9)
17 Soldier mostly going round with senior bureaucrat (8)
18 Old aunt, originally in Eccles, changing fuse (8)
21 Vessel goes round island for pleasure trip (6)
22 Raise weapon and secure something small but valuable (6)
23 Mollusc ends off shell in seven days (5)
25 Head entertaining a bishop is person of great wealth (5)

144

ACROSS

1   Bird a short distance behind guy (9)
6   Succeeded in prosperous period, or bust? (5)
9   Youngster's wonderful spelling (5)
10 It charts rise of empire, and most of fall, after revolution (6,3)
11 Such a space journey was booked three years ahead (7)
12 Jack has to sort out problems, that's clear (7)
13 Whereby one's freed from matter of some gravity (6,8)
17 Marvellous direction of some SF films? (3,2,4,5)
21 On a trip, needs method to find route (7)
23 This spinner gets the wind up – second one in panic (4-3)
25 By close of play, he was dominating in partnership (9)
26 The heart, it's said, of spicy Indian cooking (5)
27 Give up and return (5)
28 Doing one's best with ease, knocking out aces from China (9)

DOWN

1   Student lacking scholarship appearing more often (8)
2   Furious when gross abridgement's swallowed by some (5)
3   Bravely accepts stewed cups of tea (5,2,2)
4   Dash up to watch Kirov's latest dancer (7)
5   Passage covering previous case (7)
6   Ask for special favour, left in "The Black Horse" (5)
7   I'm involved in reviewing our last training system (9)
8   Clean up puppy, perhaps, a cute little one (6)
14 Try to win, about to grow English type of marrow (9)
15 Like the paperwork resulting from a joint account (2-7)
16 Water a mare, maybe, before auction (5,3)
18 Children can be accommodated here for the present (7)
19 Popular shares available for immediate sale (2,5)
20 Fast food outlet for craftsman (6)
22 Injury given a twist (5)
24 Low joint causes resentment, barring outsiders (5)

This puzzle would have been the tie-breaker in the
1998 Times Crossword Championship, had it been needed

145

ACROSS

1 Stealing mail could get you this punishment (8-4)
8 Like wood left out of fire (7)
9 Such furniture in abode's converted with frequency? (4,3)
11 Wilde's was ideal to manage (7)
12 Much is fractured on one bone (7)
13 Beak holding remove's first language class (5)
14 Vegetarian food provided by liberal head (5,4)
16 Con-men opt to reform, in part (9)
19 Split is port on East side of Adriatic (5)
21 Narrow piece of land is so, having just metres in the middle (7)
23 Get put out when retiring celebrity gets annoyed (7)
24 In this part of Europe, some praise Liszt's comeback (7)
25 Sportsman who won't get ready for a contest? (7)
26 Wryly raise a smile about line for patriotic song (12)

DOWN

1 Style of chair for house (7)
2 Anger about old horse for a long period (4,3)
3 March dance (4,5)
4 Immigrant's child that is to make serious error when turning up (5)
5 Smug audacity in school (2-5)
6 Sink U-boat seen on channel (7)
7 Fine spinach dish recreated as fast food (4,3,5)
10 Explanation for sequence of events, including cloak being found on the Circle Line? (6,6)
15 Where some varnish will dry without delay (2,3,4)
17 Queen that some Australians can bear? (7)
18 Process of absorption in universe is not constant initially (7)
19 Portion of butter I had with tea cake (7)
20 Crowd's turned up before display can be mounted here (7)
22 Crawled, perhaps, before one teacher (5)

ACROSS

1 Dismisses porters engaged within tourist area (9,5)
9 Unusual fur one had never encountered before (7-2)
10 Criticise in speech I deliver (5)
11 Tie to match uniform (5)
12 Strips off nothing – dress about to drop off (2,2,5)
13 The plane turned out to be a jumbo (8)
15 Swindled man outside one race meeting (6)
17 Cut-glass chandelier five years in the making (6)
19 Name involved in charges brought against son and daughter of king (8)
22 Education, in turn, possibly leading to university call (9)
23 Consider carefully the method announced (5)
24 Dull spell, possibly, that cuts out part of the view (5)
25 Force prisoners to exercise (9)
26 University post happens to carry American money around with it (14)

DOWN

1 As I might say to my informant, I totally agree! (5,7,2)
2 That woman over the river is to get new accommodation (7)
3 Place to sit or stand (5)
4 One tending to be broke? (8)
5 Spent two notes on holiday (6)
6 Increase a reduced volume – turn sound up about a quarter (9)
7 It's obvious I had to enter the competition (7)
8 Don't look down, stay cheerful (4,4,4,2)
14 Extraordinarily strong woman to do daily work around university (9)
16 Taken in by mouth, one drink that's fresh (8)
18 Mark to withdraw from competition (7)
20 Final words in biblical book about unleavened bread (7)
21 Enchanting woman carrying money round (6)
23 Element which all the earth received, initially (5)

147

Across

1   Its contents may be set on fire (4-4)
5   Put out fare no longer new (6)
10   Island resort's noisy beach attractions? (5)
11   Engineers adding effective buttress (9)
12   Television guide produced by London Transport (4,5)
13   Dishonest person in sport (5)
14   Loathsome and questionable behaviour reported (7)
16   Hopeless party backed political protest (6)
19   Bones found in the Bay of Naples (6)
21   Complete outfit including clothes for first night (7)
23   Sort of cycle found in traffic (5)
25   Gas used by American cars abandoned by old sailors (9)
27   Over time, provide him with a cure badly needed? (9)
28   Move around front of aeroplane in part of flight (5)
29   Longs to embrace last of grandchildren in old age (6)
30   Flower head giving pleasure (8)

Down

1   Tough sailing course takes the biscuit (4,4)
2   Border poet's whiskers (9)
3   Assume one section of market is opened up (5)
4   Have reference letters painter requires (7)
6   Money collected from ruler given to politician (9)
7   Head of school, goody-goody youth (5)
8   Study about record drug increase (6)
9   Man upset and offended (6)
15   Cause of crocodile tears? One much in trouble (9)
17   Escort during French trip taking plenty of time (9)
18   Final courses put emphasis on climbing (8)
20   Expects article – was it included? (6)
21   Serving American in pub with good reason (7)
22   Reported account of division in House (6)
24   In America, bowl last of batsmen in field (5)
26   Detected by Schnozzle Durante originally (5)

Across

1   Use it to wash down cake? (6)
5   Need to have match around in darkness (8)
9   Boastful bagpiper will do it, for a start (8)
10 Unbroken horse fit for breeding (6)
11 Fit to race about over grass (8)
12 Inclined to be concerned with special need (8)
13 Preserved and canned (7)
16 Canoe at sea, islands receding, and near deep water (7)
20 Surpass in valour, it turns out (8)
22 Primary and first form (8)
23 Badly made of wood, with crack on outside (6)
24 Allowed to tuck into chosen course – game (8)
25 Fillets securing bun with masses of hair (8)
26 What's concealing this fastening device? Quite the reverse (6)

Down

2   Vegetable set round portion of game (6)
3   The latest summit's misleading language (Blair's, actually) (8)
4   Scriptwriter (8)
5   Head for dock, going in close to berth area (7)
6   Colt's lead – a head or neck (8)
7   Would Marx have described this as a popular religious resort? (5,3)
8   A clue right off? Miraculous! (10)
12 Top GP accepting drug produces severe wind (4,6)
14 Labour's leader to add the finishing touches (3,2,3)
15 Capital part actor's given by author (8)
17 Missile-launcher delivering a light strike, in a fashion (8)
18 A police force covering international trial of crucial importance (4,4)
19 Girl learning to hack into computer system (7)
21 A free broadcasting service – relatively speaking (6)

ACROSS

1 Chief US agents sent back, being behind the times (7)
5 Enclosed area near stern that is needed in the main (7)
9 Letter or card (9)
10 Excessive force used to keep peace? Exactly! (5)
11 Play part of Phaedra, maybe (5)
12 Food supplies divided by the Spanish family (9)
14 Safety device destroyer used on exercises (7-7)
17 One achieves transfer of power by revolutionary means (9,5)
21 Restaurant Samuel Smiles would have recommended? (9)
23 Not qualified, so to speak (5)
24 Jelly made from pork or beef (5)
25 In vain, having love? (9)
26 Revolutionary principle that's fundamental (7)
27 People from colonies one sees a lot of (7)

DOWN

1 Agree to take notes (6)
2 Tea ready? I will get the bread (7)
3 A heavy depositor in Swiss banks? (9)
4 Steel band used to make this track (11)
5 Golly! This king is splendid! (3)
6 Impudence from upper layer of society (5)
7 Security device to keep squatters out? (7)
8 A ruse concocted in attempt to get funds (8)
13 Seaman protected by Republican advocate of freedom (11)
15 Tax due she recklessly spent (9)
16 It ensures one's words are discreet, so to speak (5-3)
18 Casual cricket side needing help (7)
19 Viability of attack on point of coast (7)
20 Little credit to academic stream in crucial period (6)
22 Shot in the arm, given medical treatment (5)
25 Drink up, mate! (3)

150

ACROSS

1 Missionary from state capital (5,4)
6 King Lear confused about outstanding horse (5)
9 Make an impact as one politician in general election, initially (7)
10 Girl's name, I reveal, has changed (7)
11 Author bringing happiness to church (5)
12 Lousy tune composed in insubstantial way (9)
13 Last employers? Nonsense! (8)
15 Close pen (4)
19 Speculator without female partner (4)
20 Behave arrogantly as energetic person acquiring pit (8)
23 The plight of those intending to form union (9)
24 King right to appear on a kingdom's coin (5)
26 Reformed characters given a scolding by beak (7)
27 Feller's party turn – cutting female more or less in half? (7)
28 Navigator and physicist (5)
29 Religious court had sinner converted (9)

DOWN

1 Fish jump over sailors (9)
2 Beheaded with no difficulty? That's mean (5)
3 Fondly propose to girl matrimony, finally (8)
4 Opening that makes negative changes possible (8)
5 Amorous girl in extended embrace (6)
6 A character created by 11 is blossoming (6)
7 It gives one a bit of an edge, by the way (9)
8 Song of lament, say, in cathedral city (5)
14 Old boy turning up at school in this form of transport (4-5)
16 At a grand assembly, name heroic swordsman (9)
17 Understand nothing new, hence perform badly in test? (6,2)
18 Ticks one off, providing reason for absence (4,4)
21 Cheery sound associated with 28 (6)
22 Old rhymer or modern poet (6)
23 European composer taking in English seaside attraction (5)
25 Seafood consumed by sailor merrily (5)

151

ACROSS

1 Complained as hair turned grey (8)
5 Accepted it's a sin (6)
10 So-called Pope digesting scripture slowly (5)
11 Soldier mostly working with one in hardship (9)
12 Skulduggery as old painting's considered by restorers? (5,4)
13 Piece of information workers discovered during current stoppage (5)
14 Outdoes students generally, returning star mark (7)
16 Showed fury as editor edited (6)
19 He won't accept a measure of fine quality (6)
21 Roman general with a vice, we hear (7)
23 A mate involving pawn capture comes as shock (5)
25 Claim there's no time to tuck into cheese in restaurant (9)
27 Signs of aging in Conservative ranks shown by measure (5,4)
28 Whale noise initially captured by instrument picking up sound (5)
29 Made fun of being badly dressed (6)
30 In summary, university is very dear (8)

DOWN

1 It's rarely valuable (4,4)
2 Not knowing or caring, one blunders (9)
3 Unknowns holding fortune in foreign currency (5)
4 Capitalise on stunt (7)
6 It afforded noblemen a progressive education (5,4)
7 Uplifting material for poet (5)
8 Energetic worker needing Monday off (6)
9 Argue as motorcyclist hems in front of car (6)
15 Straw bedding in empty pasture to hold a sick animal (9)
17 Naturally, nobody uses it in speech (9)
18 Offhand gesture of affection concealing extremes of love (8)
20 Physio needed in a succession of games (6)
21 List of work round flat put up – one's doing a conversion (7)
22 Relish resistance as cupholder (6)
24 One of those in sharp row may come up with a mouthful (5)
26 Author climbing this small tree (5)

ACROSS

1   Struggle to suppress counterattack (9)
6   Not initially frozen stiff (5)
9   Medicinal plant missing a long time (7)
10   Arsenal is club, perhaps, that's succeeded (7)
11   Ham beginning to go off after a short time (5)
12   In disorderly tumult, I am making final offer (9)
14   Result of love between partners? (3)
15   I direct boat, after working out observations made in passing (6,5)
17   Align people in pictures, showing understanding (11)
19   Rescue craft's depleted state (3)
20   Chap also holding young reporter back in remote place (9)
22   Section of bone found in ancient city (5)
24   Tendency to omit one of the fundamentals from education (7)
26   Any time change could be a useful feature (7)
27   A queen may be so spiteful (5)
28   Gambler has a change of heart, becoming a mere observer (9)

DOWN

1   Newspaper carrying expert view (5)
2   Man, a Scot, employed in plant (7)
3   It makes one try to land (9)
4   Comedy to suit your taste (2,3,4,2)
5   Signal heard in garden suburb (3)
6   A lot of writing about learner's field of study (5)
7   Having knowledge of alteration in costing (7)
8   Is English doctor found in unenlightened land? (9)
13   As said when fulfilling request, I knew that would happen! (5,3,3)
14   Know-all swots up about fiction (5,4)
16   Catch crossing border – what's the harm in that? (9)
18   Standing on hindlegs makes sheep breathe quickly (7)
19   Person taking an unusually soulful view of things? (7)
21   Concert that's top-class – it's in US city (5)
23   Capital leader making soldiers blossom initially (5)
25   Too much idle talk? Hang up (3)

153

ACROSS

1 Primate's sign to bishop in recess (8)
5 Against odds, precipitate fall produces injury (6)
9 Where dispensers work fast, limiting damage (8)
10 Fuss kicked up by animal welfarists in a rut? (6)
12 Soak going downhill fast? (5)
13 Charmed Eastern fellow rejected by *Times* boss (9)
14 Work leaders of Lithuania and Latvia share equally? (2,5-5)
18 Greener politician with Foreign Office installed civilian in barracks (4-8)
21 A newspaper taking writer over American Supreme Court (9)
23 An opening for theatre critic once (5)
24 Strong drink making bachelor concupiscent (6)
25 Relaxing treatment priest's given by the others (4-4)
26 Team unruffled by English league (6)
27 Star seen in East, perhaps, by chance (8)

DOWN

1 Through deceptive manoeuvre, get skirt (6)
2 One takes steps to execute Choctaws and Mohawks (6)
3 Mine is no threat to such material (9)
4 Trace development in one scientific study or another (12)
6 God producing change of heart in philosopher (5)
7 Display skill flying machines (8)
8 No bundles of banknotes ever received in these times (8)
11 Prudence of amusing person going round America on English ship (12)
15 Female soldiers covering port (9)
16 Order to take off immediately and climb (8)
17 Current measure from a politician covering drug craze (8)
19 Dog left university, carried by so-called writer (6)
20 Ornament little boy dropped into stream (6)
22 Organiser of military service (5)

154

ACROSS

1 It's why, perhaps, heart is overactive (5)
4 Site of Festival of Britain, so to speak (9)
9 Underwriter's a dreadfully arrogant upstart (9)
10 Very silly person reversing in middle of main road (5)
11 Regress, as people do, in the autumns of their years (3,3,5,4)
12 Jumbo has people in semi confusion (7)
14 Demanding English bloke gets put on team (7)
16 Maybe potter about when going back on pitch (7)
19 Weary fellow with fever taking temperature with one (7)
21 Nourishment found in desert? Really! (3,8,4)
23 Vehicle for carrying odds and ends (5)
24 Possibly gin and tonic's old name, one might assume (9)
25 Curse head of school at start of last term (9)
26 Young member of family bound to name-drop (5)

DOWN

1 Peak seen on a trip by train (4,5)
2 So-called cool cat in shades? One of them (7)
3 Stretch pullover finally over a head (5)
4 Part of Anthea's paper (7)
5 French dish cooked in port in Yorkshire area (7)
6 Visibly angered over tip given in bar (9)
7 "This is far too optimistic" a girl scoffed (7)
8 Wine I dropped in lift (5)
13 American unfamiliar with term for cricket ball (3,6)
15 Piece of film music – number one tune? (5,4)
17 About to drive off tee, finally send in different direction (2-5)
18 Baton and fiddle given to old composer (7)
19 Having a short coat taken to the cleaners (7)
20 Girl initially comparatively slow? One's putty in his hands (7)
21 Lots of honours announced (5)
22 Tales handed down – written up, likewise (5)

155

ACROSS

1 Course picked up by detective (7,4)
7 Reported excessive speed (3)
9 Catch fish moving in a small stream (9)
10 Propose to offer accommodation (3,2)
11 After study, order companion (7)
12 I record going in to hear a series of Greek tragedies (7)
13 Was dependent, having thin time (5)
15 Where to put plaster, having to use excessive stock? (9)
17 Poet is to drop round when president receives king (9)
19 Worry over issue (5)
20 Take away place I book in small coach (7)
22 Poorly, can't help out – indigestion remedy needed (7)
24 Gallant gentleman, one implicated in conspiracy (5)
25 Expression of opinion to the left of our correspondents (9)
27 Cure for effect of mild sunburn (3)
28 Horribly behind with tricky input, but finish off early (3,2,3,3)

DOWN

1 Devised series of games (3)
2 Star group performing outside port (5)
3 Date extract (4,3)
4 Deal, perhaps, going nowhere in particular (9)
5 Metal (not lead) obtained in this form? (5)
6 Very funny first line replaced by quiet poet (7)
7 Tricky situation, breaking a top tooth – might it have been chipped? (3,6)
8 Goldsmith's teacher was certainly not so frivolous (5-6)
11 Little consolation for Flora on this farm (4,7)
14 Died away from place in Yorkshire – in American cemetery (9)
16 Nobleness shown by architect's plan (9)
18 Singer formally dressed? (7)
19 Arrange to marry one March – it's nonsense to intervene (7)
21 Farm animal sticking hard in ooze (5)
23 Get up, taking care at first with leg (5)
26 Form of illumination provided guidance (3)

Note: This crossword first appeared on Christmas Eve, 1998

ACROSS

1 Promise to take wife out in friendly setting – not too dear ... (10)
7 ... large drink brought over for a quid? (4)
10 Confused as I can't grasp ultimate character of a verse-form (8)
11 Officer impounds jalopy, extremely 1*ac* (6)
12 A spot of gloom in underground coach, before starting (6)
13 Convoluted patterns seen in part of church (8)
15 Firstborn a ruse improperly deprived of right (4)
16 Whence the first 9 came to defeat expert (4,6)
18 Protest as ministers do? (4-2-4)
21 Start to 6 in delight, being recently out of pocket? (4)
22 Boz as artist with pen? (8)
24 Make a bloomer like this, and get irritable (6)
25 Lack of source for part of *A Christmas Carol*? (6)
26 Standard charge (8)
27 Act as 9 might, having forgotten first relative (4)
28 Unacceptably emphasise tax – too much (10)

DOWN

2 Inability to cope with progress revealed by final 9? (6,5)
3 Runs amok with a bock in German city (9)
4 Halts what 22*ac* does at university (5,2)
5 Support to pay single creditor, making fresh start (4,2,6,3)
6 Show surprise as I tucked into shellfish once? (7)
8 Allow to stay or go (5)
9 Spirit of Christmas for a Dickensian character (5)
14 Order what second 9 displayed with limbs (7,4)
17 Thus, with most of tour over at last, I'll stay for a while (9)
19 Tragic character, too distraught to accept dire situation (7)
20 Soused, about to collapse in European capital (7)
22 He's supposed to present tonight's awards (5)
23 First name of Dickens character called Winkle? Look into it! (5)

157

ACROSS

1 Foreign character is in the money – high living for him (7)
5 Sound of cat, one going round behind church – high-pitched sound (7)
9 New resort suffering severe blow (9)
10 Like pipe giving bath a litre (5)
11 After search, carry off gun (5)
12 Like pigs holding up rodent (9)
13 As player who's best at small part, be impatient to start acting (5,2,3,3)
17 Manufacturer on river, one who's competitive (13)
21 Equipment as put out when soldier goes in (9)
24 Specially trained horse breaking into gallop, ace runner (5)
25 In sudden movement, ring is snatched from room (5)
26 Bar snack? (9)
27 Why late is bad – early makes you this (7)
28 Like a purification ceremony artist left after deadly sin (7)

DOWN

1 Plain sort of pear, almost desiccated inside (6)
2 Like Jacob, in more ways than one (4-5)
3 Article on sex-appeal this girl shows (7)
4 Opener apt to get excited, finding what's in envelope (9)
5 Job dispatching one East as nurse for relative (5)
6 Really international woman (2,5)
7 Religious leader's interminable chatter (5)
8 Small tree tot confused with maple (8)
14 Despicable person's minion liable to poison one (9)
15 City person presiding, allowing invalid motion? (4,5)
16 Don't permit little girl to get sickly-looking (8)
18 Instrument of the devil (7)
19 Wicked and mischievous child promises to make recompense (7)
20 Painful experience in the mouth around edges of denture (6)
22 Chinese native showing extremes of paranoia (5)
23 Vulgar set? No (5)

ACROSS

1 Till unpleasant job is done, and beer runs out? (2,3,6,3)
9 Newly clean home that blends into surroundings (9)
10 Influenced by a measure taken by monarch (5)
11 On edge, extremely pushy and insolent (5)
12 Again put down people for athletic event (5,4)
13 Noticed a year on stamp is fading (4,4)
15 Rabbit food (6)
17 Working at high speed for a charge (6)
19 Make me endlessly remain a servant (8)
22 Joined up with former partner for rambling (9)
23 Works of art Roman chap and you collected (5)
24 Write off to American for a sum (5)
25 Financial expert to become involved with incomes (9)
26 Intriguing garment that hides arm also (5-3-6)

DOWN

1 Very pleased to find how trout may be caught and killed (7,2,5)
2 Walk wearily in organised parties (7)
3 Time one may have to kill (5)
4 Reserve the best for last at dinner, perhaps (3,5)
5 Confusion is no good in story (6)
6 Cash earned by Duchamp exhibit (5-4)
7 Really like the lion's share? (3,4)
8 Long for romance? Not in this film (5,9)
14 Largest island in a lake in European country (9)
16 Prophesied, giving warning, and rang bell for all to hear (8)
18 Extremely gripping concert's opening with it? (7)
20 Reversing out of side road (7)
21 Pictures put back in same niche (6)
23 One taking a bow for performance in Shakespearean role (5)

ACROSS

1 Remarkable auxiliary ecclesiastic (13)
9 Shells, for example, recycled in a fertiliser ingredient (7)
10 Sales pitch must have point to get regular order (7)
11 Plant in groups, we are told (5)
12 Short Spanish king and English queen flirt (9)
13 Outstanding English policeman in an emergency (8)
15 Contract for psychiatrist (6)
18 Bishop wary, sounding unclear (6)
19 Fascinating tricks presented without safety measure (8)
22 Foundations laid down, start a bus complex (9)
24 Sad song in calamitous key (5)
25 Unsporting? Not this game (7)
26 Get rid of high responsibility (7)
27 Hit by wave, he goes on working (6-7)

DOWN

1 Test most of legal argument, for instance (7)
2 Plate semi-developed in such photography (4-5)
3 Times taken by queen? That's appropriate (5)
4 Prepare a disguise to come on stage again (8)
5 One married couple becoming blunt (6)
6 Fur most of the stars presented to ruler (9)
7 Return and bow (5)
8 Cover girl in a thousand (6)
14 Title role for a cautious type (9)
16 Left with one trick badly needed, stick together (9)
17 Tom, perhaps, has a curry in cellar (8)
18 With bitter leaders, party split down the middle (6)
20 Ibsen's heroine tucked into ends of cracker and cheese (7)
21 Time in piece of music acceptable for composer (6)
23 Heaven for the family in *Hay Fever* (5)
24 Author, in spite of editors, taken up (5)

ACROSS

1 Method of controlling light, originally invented in lab (8,5)
9 Different part attached to a new driver (7)
10 Shot office worker during a race meeting (7)
11 Flower heads very easy to cultivate here (5)
12 Like some maths taught in elementary forms (9)
13 Resolute supporter of law reform in foundation (8)
15 Girl takes line over land to ship (6)
18 Ceasefire nicely encapsulates peacemaking (6)
19 Longing for one to be put in the picture (8)
22 Lawbreaker left to replace Jack in dance (9)
24 Scholar has to study English philosopher (5)
25 Miniature set showing play about Greek maiden (7)
26 Heron is unusual in coastal waters (7)
27 Managed to cut corner after corner, yet finish the job properly (2,3,5,3)

DOWN

1 In relation to travel document endlessly duplicated (3-1-3)
2 Probationary period of 30 days? I scoffed about it (9)
3 Light burden for a lover? (5)
4 Symbolic tale of a parrot carrying on (8)
5 Warning signal changed as one cab appears (6)
6 Where water supply can be found, by and large (2,3,4)
7 Don't agree with modest cut (5)
8 Made so difficult, by gum! (6)
14 This could be demolished with a bite (9)
16 Minimal garment – see large number in short length (9)
17 Lydia's flag (8)
18 Trick that's taking in pedestrian given a lift (6)
20 Drinks quite a lot of English herbal remedy (7)
21 A mark put on tree that's on fire (6)
23 Strip, though no good comes of it (5)
24 Associate of Don in Essex town? (5)

THE SOLUTIONS

SOLUTIONS

1

```
R O S E █ I S I S █ T O P U P
E   K   B   A   N   U   A   R
B O U Q U E T █ A I N T R E E
U   L   S   U   P   B   T   B
F U L L M A R K S █ R H Y M E
F       A   N   H   I   L   N
S A V A N T █ W O O D W I N D
█   I   S   E   T   G   N   █
B A C K H A N D █ R E C E S S
E   E   O   G   S   W       I
N A V E L █ O N T H E B A L L
E   E   I   R   A   L   M   E
F I R E D O G █ B A L L O O N
I   S   A   E   L   S   U   C
T R A C Y █ D I E T █ U R G E
```

2

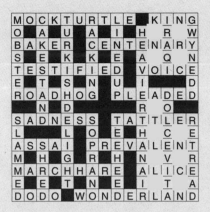

```
M O C K T U R T L E █ K I N G
O   A   U   A   I   H   R   W
B A K E R █ C E N T E N A R Y
S   E   K   K   E   A   Q   N
T E S T I F I E D █ V O I C E
E   T   S   N   U   I       D
R O A D H O G █ P L E A D E D
█   N   D       R   O       █
S A D N E S S █ T A T T L E R
L   L   O   E   H   C   E
A S S A I █ P R E V A L E N T
M   H   G   R   H   N   V   R
M A R C H H A R E █ A L I C E
E   E   T   N   E   I   T   A
D O D O █ W O N D E R L A N D
```

3

```
P U P A █ A D A M S A P P L E
E   O   D   E   A   P   S   N
S E L F A D V A N C E M E N T
T   I   T   O   X   R   U   R
O B S T A C L E █ B I R D I E
█   H   U   C   T       N   █
F I O R D █ T A L K I N G T O
O   F   E   I   A   F   O   U
L I F E S T O R Y █ S C O T S
K       D   N   P       D
M I C K E Y █ H I S P A N I C
U   H   M   S   G   R   I   H
S L I P O F T H E T O N G U E
I   L   N   U   O   M   H   A
C O L L A R B O N E █ A T O P
```

4

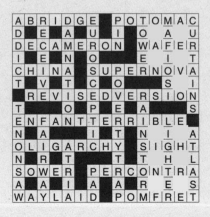

```
A B R I D G E █ P O T O M A C
D   E   A   U   I   O   A   U
D E C A M E R O N █ W A F E R
I   E   N   O       E   I   T
C H I N A █ S U P E R N O V A
T   V   T   C   O       S   I
█ R E V I S E D V E R S I O N
T   O   P   E   A       S   █
E N F A N T T E R R I B L E █
N   A   I   T   N   I   A
O L I G A R C H Y █ S I G H T
N   R   T   T       T   H   L
S O W E R █ P E R C O N T R A
A   A   I   A   A   R   E   S
W A Y L A I D █ P O M F R E T
```

5

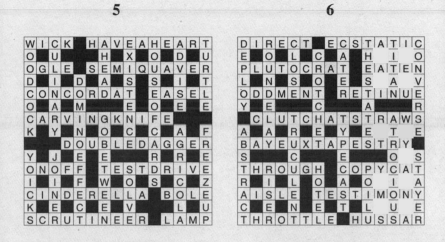

```
W I C K   H A V E A H E A R T
O U     H X   O   D U
O G L E   S E M I Q U A V E R
D   I D A S S I T
C O N C O R D A T   E A S E L
O A M   E O E E
C A R V I N G K N I F E
K Y N O C C A F
    D O U B L E D A G G E R
Y J E E R R E
O N O F F T E S T D R I V E
I I F W O S C Z
C I N D E R E L L A B O L E
K E C E V L U
S C R U T I N E E R L A M P
```

6

```
D I R E C T   E C S T A T I C
E O L C A H I O
P L U T O C R A T E A T E N
L N S O E S A V
O D D M E N T R E T I N U E
Y E C A R
  C L U T C H A T S T R A W S
A A R E Y E T E
B A Y E U X T A P E S T R Y
S C E O S
T H R O U G H C O P Y C A T
R I L O A O I A
A I S L E T E S T I M O N Y
C E N E T L U E
T H R O T T L E   H U S S A R
```

7

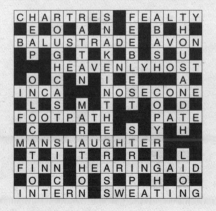

```
C H A R T R E S   F E A L T Y
E O A N E B H
B A L U S T R A D E A V O N
P G T K B S U
H E A V E N L Y H O S T
O C N I E A
I N C A N O S E C O N E
L S M T T O D
F O O T P A T H P A T E
C R E S Y H
M A N S L A U G H T E R
T I T R R I L
F I N N H E A R I N G A I D
O C O S P H O
I N T E R N S W E A T I N G
```

8

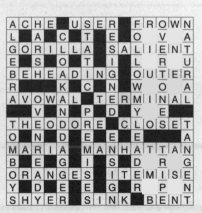

```
A C H E   U S E R   F R O W N
L A C T E O V A
G O R I L L A S A L I E N T
E S O T I L R U
B E H E A D I N G O U T E R
R K C N W O A
A V O W A L T E R M I N A L
V N P D Y E
T H E O D O R E C L O S E T
O N D E E E A
M A R I A M A N H A T T A N
B E G I S D R G
O R A N G E S I T E M I S E
Y D E E G R P N
S H Y E R S I N K   B E N T
```

SOLUTIONS

9

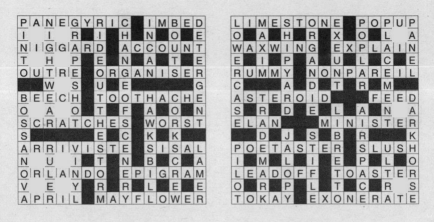

10

11

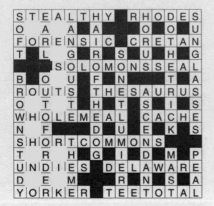

12

13

```
CARDSHARP BEBOP
L U T   R R A O E
ARGUE OBEISANCE
S B V U C I A L
SHYNESS ELLIPSE
I D E D A R
FORGOODMEASURE
Y O R W T S
 SUPERCONTINENT
A N A E N I
RADDLED BABYLON
D H A D U E G
OVERSPILL RAVER
U A S S A N E A
RODEO HORSEPLAY
```

14

```
FABRIC APERITIF
P A A R E R L
SPEC TAKEITEASY
A K C S A D W
BREECH PEDICURE
E T U N N C I
PLAYAPART EYING
O N S F E R N H
LEGIT FORESIGHT
I E R L N G O
SYLLABUS VANDAL
H I D E E O R
OCCIDENTAL BODY
F A L C O L E
FALTERED POETRY
```

15

```
PASTE CELLARAGE
A A X O U M N W
LATECOMER AGATE
I I I C T E R
MEALSONWHEELS
P P E T U T S
SEPT MEMBERSHIP
E R S R U S E I
SHORTENING USER
T P A T S I I
 ROGUEELEPHANT
A I N N I I L
DRAMA SANATORIA
Z T N U E E I M
ELECTRESS DROOP
```

16

```
MARMOT CANAILLE
G A E L O G E
BROKENDOWN LIFT
E E A U U O T
REASONED SPOTON
H T C A V
MALI UNGLOVED
G F B C E F R
BOATHOOK FIST
N T O S T
BYPASS OVERHANG
A R W L N E Y
BUNG ADAMSAPPLE
N O N N O E O
STANDARD REGENT
```

SOLUTIONS

17

18

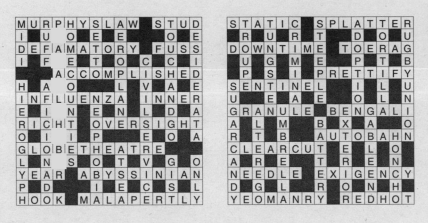

19

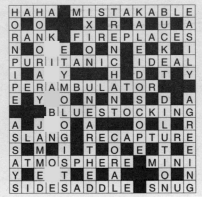

20

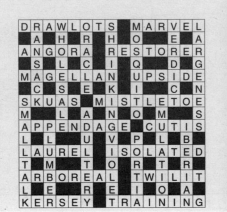

21

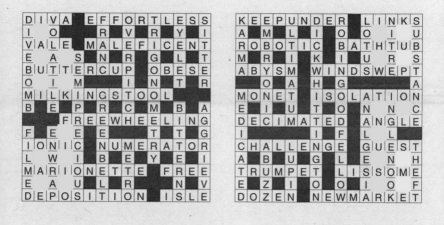

```
D I V A   E F F O R T L E S S
I   O     R   V   R   Y     I
V A L E   M A L E F I C E N T
E   A S   N   R   G   L     T
B U T T E R C U P   O B E S E
O   I M     I   N   T     R
M I L K I N G S T O O L
B   E   P   R   C   M   B A
    F R E E W H E E L I N G
F E E   E     T   T     T G
I O N I C   N U M E R A T O R
L   W   I   B   E   Y   E   I
M A R I O N E T T E   F R E E
E   A U   L   R       N     V
D E P O S I T I O N   I S L E
```

22

```
K E E P U N D E R   L I N K S
A   M   L   I   O   O   I   U
R O B O T I C   B A T H T U B
M   R   I   K   I   U   R   S
A B Y S M   W I N D S W E P T
    O   A   H   G       A
M O N E T   I S O L A T I O N
E   I   U   T   O   N   N   C
D E C I M A T E D   A N G L E
I       I   F   L   L
C H A L L E N G E   G U E S T
A   B U G   L   E   N     H
T R U M P E T   L I S S O M E
E   Z   I   O   O   I   O F
D O Z E N   N E W M A R K E T
```

23

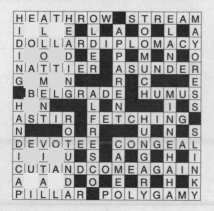

```
H E A T H R O W   S T R E A M
I   L   E   L   A   O   L   A
D O L L A R D I P L O M A C Y
I   O   D   E   P   M   N   O
N A T T I E R   A S U N D E R
G   M   N       R   C     E
  B E L G R A D E   H U M U S
H   N     L   N       I   S
A S T I R   F E T C H I N G
N     O   R     U   N   S
D E V O T E E   C O N G E A L
I   I   U   S   A   G   H   I
C U T A N D C O M E A G A I N
A   A   D   O   E   R   H   K
P I L L A R   P O L Y G A M Y
```

24

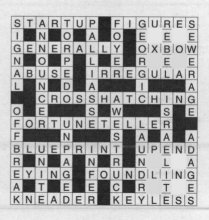

```
S T A R T U P   F I G U R E S
I   N   O   A   O   E   E   E
G E N E R A L L Y   O X B O W
N   O   P   L   E   R   E   E
A B U S E   I R R E G U L A R
L   N   D   A   I       A
    C R O S S H A T C H I N G
O   E   S   W       S     E
F O R T U N E T E L L E R
F   N     S   A   A   A   A
B L U E P R I N T   U P E N D
R   N   A   N   R   N   L A
E Y I N G   F O U N D L I N G
A   T   E   E   C   R   T E
K N E A D E R   K E Y L E S S
```

SOLUTIONS

25

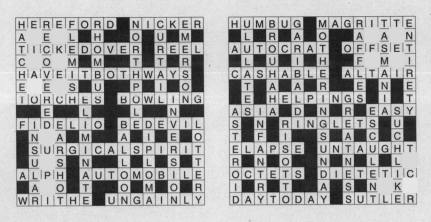

26

27

28

29

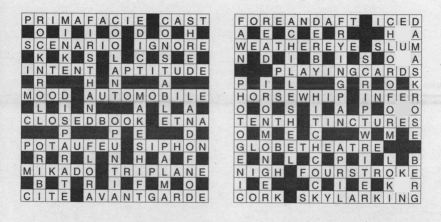

```
P R I M A F A C I E   C A S T
  O   I   I   O   D   O   H
S C E N A R I O   I G N O R E
  K   K   S   L   C   S   E
I N T E N T   A P T I T U D E
  R   H   N   A       A
M O O D   A U T O M O B I L E
  L   I   N   A   L   A
C L O S E D B O O K   E T N A
      P       P   E   D
P O T A U F E U   S I P H O N
  R   R   L   N   H   A   F
M I K A D O   T R I P L A N E
  B   T   R   I   F   M   O
C I T E   A V A N T G A R D E
```

30

```
F O R E A N D A F T   I C E D
A   E   C   E   R   H   A
W E A T H E R E Y E   S L U M
N   D   I   B   I   S   O   A
      P L A Y I N G C A R D S
P   I   L   G   R   O   K
H O R S E W H I P   I N F E R
O   O   S   I   A   P   O   O
T E N T H   T I N C T U R E S
O   M   E   C       W   M   E
G L O B E T H E A T R E
E   N   L   C   P   I   L   B
N I G H   F O U R S T R O K E
I   E       C   I   E   K   R
C O R K   S K Y L A R K I N G
```

31

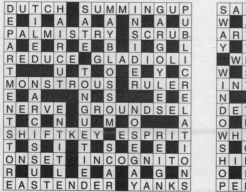

```
D U T C H   S U M M I N G U P
E   I   A   A   N   A   U
P A L M I S T R Y   S C R U B
A   E   R   E   B   I   G   L
R E D U C E   G L A D I O L I
T   U   T   O   E   Y   C
M O N S T R O U S   R U L E R
E   A   N   S   S   E   E
N E R V E   G R O U N D S E L
T   C   N   U   M   O   A
S H I F T K E Y   E S P R I T
T   S   I   T   S   E   E   I
O N S E T   I N C O G N I T O
R   U   L   E   A   G   N
E A S T E N D E R   Y A N K S
```

32

```
S A F A R I P A R K   O S L O
W   A   I   O   E   E   V
A R T I C U L A T E   G A M E
Y   T   H   E   O   S   C   R
  W E S T   S T R I K E O U T
W   S   E   T   T   A   O   H
I N T E R V A L   S T O K E R
N   S   R   D   E   E   O
D E T A C H   D U M B S H O W
O   R   A   S   B   O   A   N
W H I R L P O O L   A R G O
S   C   E   U   I   R   G   W
H I K E   G R A N A D I L L A
O   L   C   E   E   E   L   A
P E E R   T E R R O R I S E D
```

SOLUTIONS

33

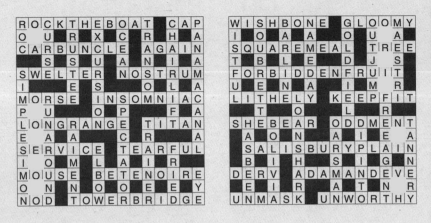

```
R O C K T H E B O A T   C A P
O U   R X   C   R   H   A
C A R B U N C L E   A G A I N
  S   S U   A   N   I   A
S W E L T E R   N O S T R U M
I   E   S   O   L   A
M O R S E   I N S O M N I A C
P U   O   P   F   A
L O N G R A N G E   T I T A N
E A   A   C   R   A
S E R V I C E   T E A R F U L
I O   M   L   I   R
M O U S E   B E T E N O I R E
O N   N O   O   E   E Y
N O D   T O W E R B R I D G E
```

34

```
W I S H B O N E   G L O O M Y
I O   A   A   O   U   A
S Q U A R E M E A L   T R E E
T   B   L   E   D   J   S
F O R B I D D E N F R U I T
U E   N   A   I   M   R
L I T H E L Y   K E E P F I T
E   T   O   L   R
S H E B E A R   O D D M E N T
  A O   N   A   I   E   A
  S A L I S B U R Y P L A I N
  B   I   H   S   I   G   N
D E R V   A D A M A N D E V E
E   I   R   A   T   N   R
U N M A S K   U N W O R T H Y
```

35

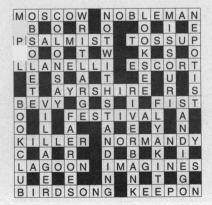

```
M O S C O W   N O B L E M A N
  B   O   R   O   I   E
P S A L M I S T   T O S S U P
  O   O   T   W   K   S   O
L L A N E L L I   E S C O R T
  E   S   A   T   E   U   I
  T   A Y R S H I R E   R   S
B E V Y   G   S   I   F I S T
O   I   F E S T I V A L   A
O   L   A   A   E   Y   N
K I L L E R   N O R M A N D Y
C   A   R   D   B   K   I
L A G O O N   I M A G I N E S
U   E   E   N   N   T   G
B I R D S O N G   K E E P O N
```

36

```
  U P T O T H E M I N U T E
N   H   A   V   N   N   L
I D L E   R A I S E   C R E W
E   T   N   C   P   O   C
O R G A N I S T   T R U S T Y
T   S   O   P   R
W H I T E H O R S E   L A I D
E   E   E   V   E   C
S C U T   D E A L E R S H I P
O   R   S   R   T
S U M A C H   E D G E W A Y S
N   G   A   P   R   E   B
S T I R   B U T T E   B R I G
E   A   I   I   E   L
R E M O T E C O N T R O L
```

37

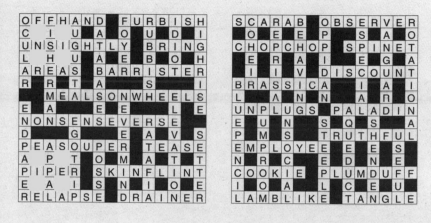

O	F	F	H	A	N	D		F	U	R	B	I	S	H
C		I		U		A		O		U		D		I
U	N	S	I	G	H	T	L	Y		B	R	I	N	G
L		H		U		A		E		B		O		H
A	R	E	A	S		B	A	R	R	I	S	T	E	R
R		R		T		A			S					I
	M	E	A	L	S	O	N	W	H	E	E	L	S	
E		A			E		E				L		E	
N	O	N	S	E	N	S	E	V	E	R	S	E		
D		G			E		A		V		S			
P	E	A	S	O	U	P	E	R		T	E	A	S	E
A		P		O		M		A		T		T		
P	I	P	E	R		S	K	I	N	F	L	I	N	T
E		A		I		S		N		I		O		E
R	E	L	A	P	S	E		D	R	A	I	N	E	R

38

S	C	A	R	A	B		O	B	S	E	R	V	E	R
	O		E		E		P		S		A		O	
C	H	O	P	C	H	O	P		S	P	I	N	E	T
	E		R		A		I		E		G		A	
	I		I		V		D	I	S	C	O	U	N	T
B	R	A	S	S	I	C	A		I		A		I	
L		A		N		N		A		R		O		
U	N	P	L	U	G	S		P	A	L	A	D	I	N
E		U		N		S		Q		S		A		
P		M		S		T	R	U	T	H	F	U	L	
E	M	P	L	O	Y	E	E		E		E		S	
N		R		C		E		D		N		E		
C	O	O	K	I	E		P	L	U	M	D	U	F	F
I		O		A		L		C		E		U		
L	A	M	B	L	I	K	E		T	A	N	G	L	E

39

T	E	L	E	S	C	O	P	E		E	N	T	E	R
U		E		C		P		X		G		E		E
R	I	V	E	R		P	A	P	E	R	C	L	I	P
N		E		A		O		L		E		E		A
D	I	L	U	T	E	S		O	C	T	O	P	U	S
O			C		E		I			H		T		
W	E	A	T	H	E	R	S	T	A	T	I	O	N	
N		L		E				A		T		A		
	C	L	A	S	S	C	O	N	S	C	I	O	U	S
I		O			O		E		K		T			
C	O	W	S	L	I	P		W	H	I	S	T	L	E
E		A		U		I		Y		N		A		R
C	O	N	T	R	A	L	T	O		E	N	N	U	I
A		C		E		O		R		S		G		S
P	L	E	A	D		T	A	K	E	S	T	O	C	K

40

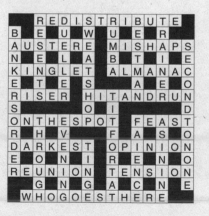

	R	E	D	I	S	T	R	I	B	U	T	E	
B		E		U		W		U		E		R	
A	U	S	T	E	R	E		M	I	S	H	A	P	S
N		E		L		A		B		T		I		E
K	I	N	G	L	E	T		A	L	M	A	N	A	C
E		T		E		S			A		E		O	
R	I	S	E	R		H	I	T	A	N	D	R	U	N
S				O		I						D	
O	N	T	H	E	S	P	O	T		F	E	A	S	T
R		H		V			F		A		S		O	
D	A	R	K	E	S	T		O	P	I	N	I	O	N
E		O		N		I		R		E		N		O
R	E	U	N	I	O	N		T	E	N	S	I	O	N
	G		N		G		A		C		N		E	
W	H	O	G	O	E	S	T	H	E	R	E	

SOLUTIONS

41

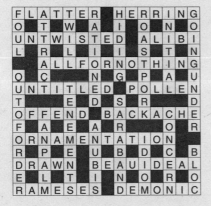

F	L	A	T	T	E	R		H	E	R	R	I	N	G
O		T		W		A		I		O		N		O
U	N	T	W	I	S	T	E	D		A	L	I	B	I
L		R		L		I		I		S		T		N
	A	L	L	F	O	R	N	O	T	H	I	N	G	
O		C		N		G		P		A			U	
U	N	T	I	T	L	E	D		P	O	L	L	E	N
T			E		D		S		R			D		
O	F	F	E	N	D		B	A	C	K	A	C	H	E
F		A		E		A		R		O		R		R
O	R	N	A	M	E	N	T	A	T	I	O	N		
R		P		E		U		B		D		C		B
D	R	A	W	N		B	E	A	U	I	D	E	A	L
E		L		T		I		N		O		R		O
R	A	M	E	S	E	S		D	E	M	O	N	I	C

42

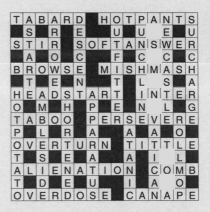

T	A	B	A	R	D		H	O	T	P	A	N	T	S
	S		R		E		U		U		E		U	
S	T	I	R		S	O	F	T	A	N	S	W	E	R
	A		O		C		F		C		C		C	
B	R	O	W	S	E		M	I	S	H	M	A	S	H
	T		E		N		T		L		S		A	
H	E	A	D	S	T	A	R	T		I	N	T	E	R
O		M		H		P		E		N		L		G
T	A	B	O	O		P	E	R	S	E	V	E	R	E
P		L		R		A		A		A		O		
O	V	E	R	T	U	R	N		T	I	T	T	L	E
T		S		E		A		A		I		L		
A	L	I	E	N	A	T	I	O	N		C	O	M	B
T		D		E		U		I		A		O		
O	V	E	R	D	O	S	E		C	A	N	A	P	E

43

B	L	I	N	D	A	L	L	E	Y		B	E	T	H
L		C		R		E		L		F		A		U
O	B	E	S	E		F	L	A	M	I	N	G	O	S
O		S		S		T		S		L		E		B
M	A	K	E	S	H	I	F	T		L	A	R	V	A
E		A		R		S		I		I				N
R	E	T	R	E	A	T		C	A	N	D	I	E	D
		E		H				G		N				
B	U	R	G	E	O	N		I	N	S	E	C	T	S
E			A		U		C		T		L		E	
L	E	V	E	R		C	A	E	S	A	R	E	A	N
L		E		S		L		B		T		M		A
M	A	N	G	A	N	E	S	E		I	N	E	R	T
A		U		L		A		R		O		N		O
N	O	E	S		P	R	O	G	E	N	I	T	O	R

44

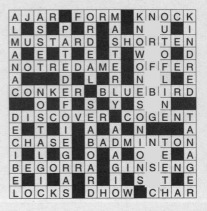

A	J	A	R		F	O	R	M		K	N	O	C	K
L		S		P		R		A		N		U		I
M	U	S	T	A	R	D		S	H	O	R	T	E	N
A		E		T		E		T		W		O		D
N	O	T	R	E	D	A	M	E		O	F	F	E	R
A			D		L		R		N		L		E	
C	O	N	K	E	R		B	L	U	E	B	I	R	D
		O		F		S		Y		S		N		
D	I	S	C	O	V	E	R		C	O	G	E	N	T
E		T		I		A		A		N				A
C	H	A	S	E		B	A	D	M	I	N	T	O	N
I		L		G		O		A		O		E		A
B	E	G	O	R	R	A		G	I	N	S	E	N	G
E		I		A		R		I		S		T		E
L	O	C	K	S		D	H	O	W		C	H	A	R

45

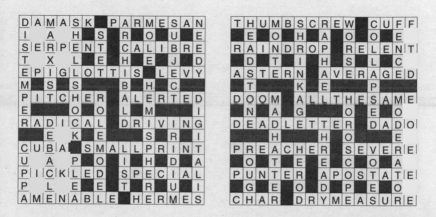

46

47

48

49

```
E N C H I L A D A S   E C H O
A   A   D   I   N     A   P
C E N T I G R A D E   A R C H
H   T   O   B   R I N   T
  M A R S   O V E R R E A C H
E   T   Y   R   W   O   G   A
L E A R N I N G   U N R E A L
E       C   E   R   I       M
C E L E R Y   S H A N G H A I
T   O   A   C   E   G   E   C
O R R I S R O O T   B O M B
R   E   Y   R   O   O   L   Z
A L L Y   T O U R M A L I N E
T   E     N   I   R   N   U
E V I L   F A N C Y D R E S S
```

50

```
C H A O S   T R E A C H E R Y
U   N   O   H   E   A   L   O
C H A U F F E U R   R E E D Y
K   T   S   I   E   C       O
O N T H E F A C E O F I T
O   O   N   U     R   R   A
P I T Y   B R O W N E D O F F
I   H   F   U   E   N       T
N E E D L E S S L Y   L I V E
T   L   A   S   S   C   R
  E N T E R T H E L I S T S
R   T   W   E   H   I       H
U L T R A   A N A L G E S I A
T   E   R   C   R   H   A   V
H O R S E W H I P   T H Y M E
```

51

```
L O O S E S T R I F E   E G G
E   R   S   A   N   L   N   E
I D E N T I K I T   A N G E R
    A   U   E   R   S   I   M
E N D E A R S   O U T G R O W
X       R   O   I   D   A
T O D A Y   V E H I C U L A R
E   R       E   O   E   F
M O U S E T R A P   P O D I A
P   M   R   S   E       R
O B S E R V E   C A R N A G E
R   T   A   A   O   D   N
I D I O T   G E T T I N G O N
S   C   U   E   C   T   E   O
E R K   M A R S H M A L L O W
```

52

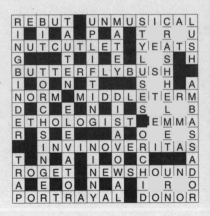

```
R E B U T   U N M U S I C A L
I   I   A   P   A   T   R   U
N U T C U T L E T   Y E A T S
G       T   I   E   L   S   H
B U T T E R F L Y B U S H
I   O   N   T   S   H   A
N O R M   M I D D L E T E R M
D   C   E   N   I   S   L   B
E T H O L O G I S T   E M M A
R   S   E   A   O   E   S
  I N V I N O V E R I T A S
T   N   A   I   O   C   A
R O G E T   N E W S H O U N D
A   E   O   N   A   I   R   O
P O R T R A Y A L   D O N O R
```

53

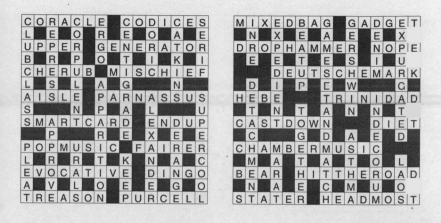

```
C O R A C L E   C O D I C E S
L   E   O   R   E   O   A   E
U P P E R   G E N E R A T O R
B   R   P   O   T   I   K   I
C H E R U B   M I S C H I E F
L   S   L   A   G       N
A I S L E   P A R N A S S U S
S   N   P   A   L       U
S M A R T C A R D   E N D U P
    P   R   E   X   E   E
P O P M U S I C   F A I R E R
L   R   R   T   K   N   A   C
E V O C A T I V E   D I N G O
A   V   L   O   E   E   G   O
T R E A S O N   P U R C E L L
```

54

```
M I X E D B A G   G A D G E T
  N   X   E   A   E   E   X
D R O P H A M M E R   N O P E
  E   E   T   E   S   I   U
    D E U T S C H E M A R K
  D   I   P   E   W       G
H E B E   T R I N I D A D
  T   N   T   A   N   N   T
C A S T D O W N   D I E T
  C   G   D   A   E   D
C H A M B E R M U S I C
  M   A   T   A   T   O   L
B E A R   H I T T H E R O A D
  N   A   E   C   M   U   O
S T A T E R   H E A D M O S T
```

55

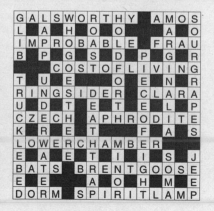

```
G A L S W O R T H Y   A M O S
L   A   H   O   O       A   O
I M P R O B A B L E   F R A U
B   P   G   S   D   P   G   R
    C O S T O F L I V I N G
T   U   E   O   E   N   R
R I N G S I D E R   C L A R A
U   D   T   E   T   E   L   P
C Z E C H   A P H R O D I T E
K   R   E   T   F   A   S
L O W E R C H A M B E R
E   A   E   T   I   I   S   J
B A T S   B R E N T G O O S E
E   E       A   O   H   M   E
D O R M   S P I R I T L A M P
```

56

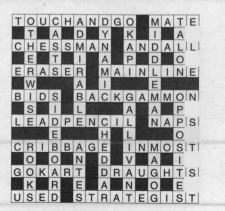

```
T O U C H A N D G O   M A T E
  T   A   D   Y   K   I   A
C H E S S M A N   A N D A L L
  E   T   I   A   P   D   O
E R A S E R   M A I N L I N E
  W   A   I       E
B I D S   B A C K G A M M O N
  S   I   L   A   A   P
L E A D P E N C I L   N A P S
  E       H   L       O
C R I B B A G E   I N M O S T
  O   O   N   D   V   A   I
G O K A R T   D R A U G H T S
  K   R   E   A   N   O   E
U S E D   S T R A T E G I S T
```

57

58

59

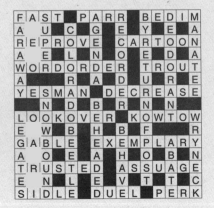

60

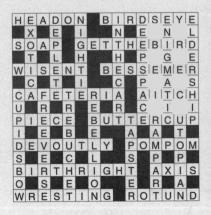

61

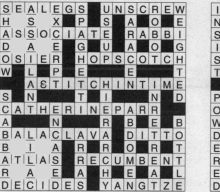

S	E	A	L	E	G	S		U	N	S	C	R	E	W
H		S	X		P		S		A		O		E	
A	S	S	O	C	I	A	T	E		R	A	B	B	I
D		A		E		G		U		A		O		G
O	S	I	E	R		H	O	P	S	C	O	T	C	H
W		L		P		E			E					T
	A	S	T	I	T	C	H	I	N	T	I	M	E	
S		N		T		I			N			N		D
C	A	T	H	E	R	I	N	E	P	A	R	R		
A			N			R		B		E		B		B
B	A	L	A	C	L	A	V	A		D	I	T	T	O
B		I		A		R		R		O		R		T
A	T	L	A	S		R	E	C	U	M	B	E	N	T
R		A		E		A		H		E		A		L
D	E	C	I	D	E	S		Y	A	N	G	T	Z	E

62

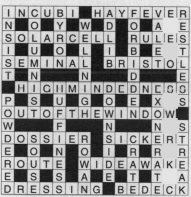

I	N	C	U	B	I		H	A	Y	F	E	V	E	R
N		O		Y		W		D		O		A		E
S	O	L	A	R	C	E	L	L		R	U	L	E	S
I		U		O		L		I		B		E		T
S	E	M	I	N	A	L		B	R	I	S	T	O	L
T		N			N			N		D				E
	H	I	G	H	M	I	N	D	E	D	N	E	S	S
P		S		U		G		O		E		X		S
O	U	T	O	F	T	H	E	W	I	N	D	O	W	
W			F			N		N				N		S
D	O	S	S	I	E	R		S	I	C	K	E	R	T
E		O		N		O		I		R		R		R
R	O	U	T	E		W	I	D	E	A	W	A	K	E
E		S		S		A		E		T		T		A
D	R	E	S	S	I	N	G		B	E	D	E	C	K

63

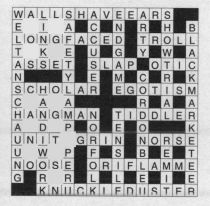

W	A	L	L	S	H	A	V	E	E	A	R	S		
E		I		A		C		N		R		H		B
L	O	N	G	F	A	C	E	D		T	R	O	L	L
T		K		E		U		G		Y		W		A
A	S	S	E	T		S	L	A	P		O	T	I	C
N			Y		E		M		C		R			K
S	C	H	O	L	A	R		E	G	O	T	I	S	M
C		A		A				R		A		A		
H	A	N	G	M	A	N		T	I	D	D	L	E	R
A		D		P		O		E		O				K
U	N	I	T		G	R	I	N		N	O	R	S	E
U		W		P		F		S		B		E		T
N	O	O	S	E		O	R	I	F	L	A	M	M	E
G		R		R		L		L		E		I		E
	K	N	U	C	K	L	E	D	U	S	T	E	R	

64

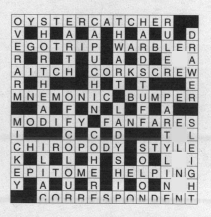

O	Y	S	T	E	R	C	A	T	C	H	E	R		
V		H		A		A		H		A		U		D
E	G	O	T	R	I	P		W	A	R	B	L	E	R
R		R		T		U		A		D		E		A
A	I	T	C	H		C	O	R	K	S	C	R	E	W
R		H		T		H		T		T				E
M	N	E	M	O	N	I	C		B	U	M	P	E	R
		A		F		N		L		F		A		
M	O	D	I	F	Y		F	A	N	F	A	R	E	S
I			C		C		D			T		L		
C	H	I	R	O	P	O	D	Y		S	T	Y	L	E
K		L		L		H		S		O		L		I
E	P	I	T	O	M	E		H	E	L	P	I	N	G
Y		A		U		R		I		O		N		H
	C	O	R	R	E	S	P	O	N	D	E	N	T	

SOLUTIONS

65

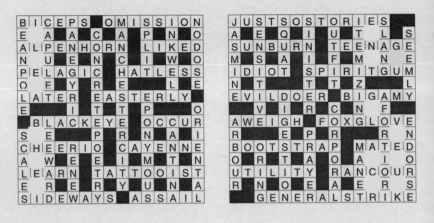

```
B I C E P S   O M I S S I O N
E   A   A   C   A   P   N   O
A L P E N H O R N   L I K E D
N   U   E   N   C   I   W   O
P E L A G I C   H A T L E S S
O   E   Y   R   E       L   E
L A T E R   E A S T E R L Y
E       I   T   T   P       O
  B L A C K E Y E   O C C U R
S   E       P   R   N   A   I
C H E E R I O   C A Y E N N E
A   W   E   E   I   M   T   N
L E A R N   T A T T O O I S T
E   R   E   R   Y   U   N   A
S I D E W A Y S   A S S A I L
```

66

```
J U S T S O S T O R I E S
A   E   Q   I   U   T   L   S
S U N B U R N   T E E N A G E
M   S   A   I   F   M   N   E
I D I O T   S P I R I T G U M
N   T       T   T   Z       L
E V I L D O E R   B I G A M Y
    V   I   R   C   N   F
A W E I G H   F O X G L O V E
R   E       P   R       R   N
B O O T S T R A P   M A T E D
O   R   T   A   O   A   I   O
U T I L I T Y   R A N C O U R
R   N   O   E   A   E   R   S
  G E N E R A L S T R I K E
```

67

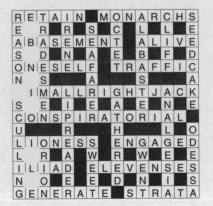

```
R E T A I N   M O N A R C H S
E   R   R   S   C   L   L   E
A B A S E M E N T   A L I V E
S   D   N   A   E   B   F   D
O N E S E L F   T R A F F I C
N   S   A       S   A
  I M A L L R I G H T J A C K
S   E   I   E   A   E   N   E
C O N S P I R A T O R I A L
U       R   H       L   O
L I O N E S S   E N G A G E D
L   R   A   W   R   W   E   E
I L I A D   E L E V E N S E S
N   O   E   E   D   N   I   S
G E N E R A T E   S T R A T A
```

68

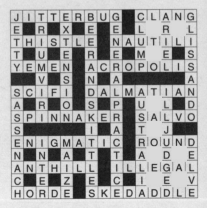

```
J I T T E R B U G   C L A N G
E   R   X   E   E   L   R   L
T H I S T L E   N A U T I L I
T   U   E   R   E   M   E   S
Y E M E N   A C R O P O L I S
    V   S   N   A       I   A
S C I F I   D A L M A T I A N
A   R   O   S   P   U   L   D
S P I N N A K E R   S A L V O
S       I   A   T   J
E N I G M A T I C   R O U N D
N   N   A   T   T   A   D   E
A N T H I L L   I L L E G A L
C   E   Z   E   C   I   E   V
H O R D E   S K E D A D D L E
```

69

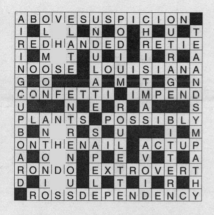

70

71

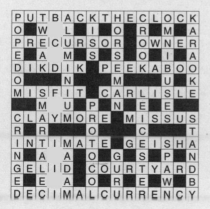

72

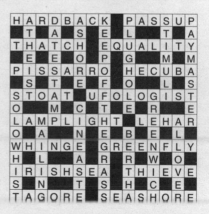

SOLUTIONS

73

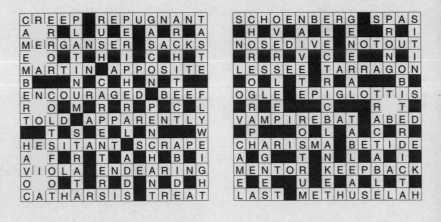

C	R	E	E	P		R	E	P	U	G	N	A	N	T
A		R		L	U	E		A		R		A		
M	E	R	G	A	N	S	E	R		S	A	C	K	S
E		O		T		H		I		C		H		T
M	A	R	T	I	N		A	P	P	O	S	I	T	E
B			N		C		H		N		T			
E	N	C	O	U	R	A	G	E	D		B	E	E	F
R		O		M		R		R		P		C		L
T	O	L	D		A	P	P	A	R	E	N	T	L	Y
		T		S		E		L		N				W
H	E	S	I	T	A	N	T		S	C	R	A	P	E
A		F		R		T		A		H		B		I
V	I	O	L	A		E	N	D	E	A	R	I	N	G
O		O		T		R		D		N		D		H
C	A	T	H	A	R	S	I	S		T	R	E	A	T

74

S	C	H	O	E	N	B	E	R	G		S	P	A	S
	H		V		A		L		E		R		I	
N	O	S	E	D	I	V	E		N	O	T	O	U	T
	R		R		V		C		E		N		I	
L	E	S	S	E	E		T	A	R	R	A	G	O	N
	O		L		T		R		A				B	
O	G	L	E		E	P	I	G	L	O	T	T	I	S
	R		E				C				R		T	
V	A	M	P	I	R	E	B	A	T		A	B	E	D
	P				O		L		A		C		R	
C	H	A	R	I	S	M	A		B	E	T	I	D	E
A		G		T		N		L		A		I		
M	E	N	T	O	R		K	E	E	P	B	A	C	K
E		E		U		E		A		L		T		
L	A	S	T		M	E	T	H	U	S	E	L	A	H

75

A	B	B	E		K	I	S	S		T	O	A	S	T
P		R		P		B		L		U		D		A
P	R	A	I	R	I	E		O	W	N	G	O	A	L
A		C		A		R		U		B		R		E
R	E	T	A	I	N	I	N	G		R	U	N	I	N
E		S		A		H		I		M		T		
L	U	G	G	E	R		N	E	E	D	L	E	S	S
		O		W		B		D		G		N		
R	O	L	L	O	V	E	R		S	E	X	T	O	N
E		D		R		W		S		W				O
A	V	E	R	T		I	N	C	R	E	A	S	E	S
D		N		H		L		O		L		P		E
M	A	R	R	I	E	D		T	E	L	L	I	N	G
I		O		L		E		E		S		K		A
T	O	D	A	Y		R	A	R	E		V	E	R	Y

76

L	I	B	R	A		S	E	N	T	E	N	C	E	D
O		A		L		T		E		U		O		U
C	O	R	K	S	C	R	E	W		L	A	M	E	D
K		A		E		E		E		O		P		S
S	A	L	E	C	A	T	A	L	O	G	U	E		
M		I		E		C		I		T		T		M
I	O	T	A		C	H	O	R	U	S	L	I	N	E
T		T		M		E		E		T		T		R
H	E	L	I	O	G	R	A	P	H		L	I	A	R
S		E		N		A		R		O				Y
	W	H	A	T	D	O	Y	O	U	K	N	O	W	
E		O		L		I		M		M				I
T	E	M	P	I		S	H	E	E	P	F	O	L	D
C		E		S		C		N		U		A		O
H	A	N	G	A	B	O	U	T		S	T	R	A	W

77

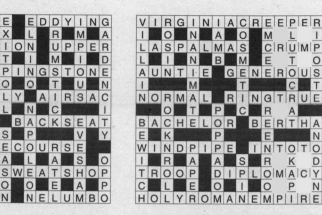

V	E	H	I	C	L	E		E	D	D	Y	I	N	G
I		O		L		X		L		R		M		A
S	A	L	V	A	T	I	O	N		U	P	P	E	R
A		Y		R		T		I		M		I		D
		S	T	E	P	P	I	N	G	S	T	O	N	E
M	E			O		O		T		U		N		
U	S	E	F	U	L	L	Y		A	I	R	S	A	C
S				N		L		N		C				I
I	N	C	H	E	S		B	A	C	K	S	E	A	T
C		H		A		S		P		V		V		Y
S	T	A	Y	T	H	E	C	O	U	R	S	E		
T		P		A		A		L		A		S		O
A	D	L	I	B		S	W	E	A	T	S	H	O	P
N		I		O		O		E		A				P
D	U	N	G	E	O	N		N	E	L	U	M	B	O

78

V	I	R	G	I	N	I	A	C	R	E	E	P	E	R
I		O		N		A		O		M		L		I
L	A	S	P	A	L	M	A	S		C	R	U	M	P
L		I		N		B		M		E		T		O
A	U	N	T	I	E		G	E	N	E	R	O	U	S
I				M				T		C		I		T
N	O	R	M	A	L		R	I	N	G	T	R	U	E
		O		T		P		C		R		A		
B	A	C	H	E	L	O	R		B	E	R	T	H	A
E		K			P		P			E				N
W	I	N	D	P	I	P	E		I	N	T	O	T	O
I		R		A		A		S		R		K		D
T	R	O	O	P		D	I	P	L	O	M	A	C	Y
C		L		E		O		I		O		P		N
H	O	L	Y	R	O	M	A	N	E	M	P	I	R	E

79

R	E	S	P	I	T	E		P	A	R	A	P	E	T
E		T		N		M		L		A		L		R
C	R	U	E	T		I	N	E	B	R	I	A	T	E
E		M		E		T		A		E		C		A
P	E	B	B	L	E		E	S	U	R	I	E	N	T
T		L		L		E		A		B				
I	R	E	N	E		X	E	N	O	P	H	O	B	E
O			C		T		T		R					X
N	I	G	H	T	B	E	L	L		I	N	S	E	T
		A		R		Y		N		H		E		
D	A	Z	Z	L	I	N	G		S	C	R	E	E	N
U		E		A		I		I		A				S
B	E	L	L	P	U	L	L	S		P	U	T	T	I
A		L		I		L		H		O				O
I	D	E	A	L	L	Y		S	H	E	B	E	E	N

80

S	A	V	E	O	N	E	S	B	A	C	O	N		
T		I		R		M		R		A		E		B
E	N	C	L	A	S	P		A	P	P	A	R	E	L
W		A		C		H		I		A		V		I
A	R	R	A	Y		A	B	S	O	R	B	E	N	T
R		I				S		E		I				H
D	O	O	R	N	A	I	L		E	S	C	A	P	E
		U		E		S		B		O		D		
D	I	S	O	W	N		T	R	A	N	S	M	I	T
E				F		P		A				I		R
C	U	S	T	O	D	I	A	N		P	A	S	T	A
I		C		R		G		D		R		S		P
D	I	O	C	E	S	E		I	D	O	L	I	S	E
E		T		S		O		S		O		O		Z
		S	I	T	O	N	T	H	E	F	E	N	C	E

SOLUTIONS

81

82

83

84

85

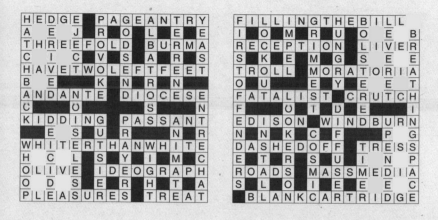

86

87

88

SOLUTIONS

89

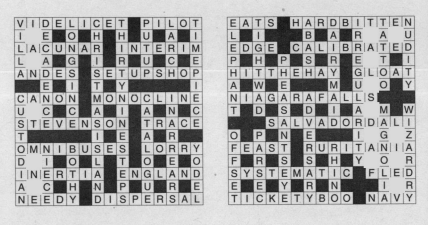

```
V I D E L I C E T   P I L O T
I   E   O   H   H   U   A   I
L A C U N A R   I N T E R I M
L   A   G   I   R   U   C   E
A N D E S   S E T U P S H O P
  E     I   T   Y       I
C A N O N   M O N O C L I N E
U   C   C   A   I   A   N   C
S T E V E N S O N   T R A C E
T       I     E   A   R
O M N I B U S E S   L O R R Y
D   I   O   L   T   O   E   O
I N E R T I A   E N G L A N D
A   C   H   N   P   U   R   E
N E E D Y   D I S P E R S A L
```

90

```
E A T S   H A R D B I T T E N
L   I     B   A   R   A   U
E D G E   C A L I B R A T E D
P   H   P   S   R   E   T   I
H I T T H E H A Y   G L O A T
A   W   E     M   U   O   Y
N I A G A R A F A L L S
T   D   S   D   I   A   M   W
    S A L V A D O R D A L I
O   P   N   E       I   G   Z
F E A S T   R U R I T A N I A
F   R   S   S   H   Y   O   R
S Y S T E M A T I C   F L E D
E   E   Y   R   N       I   R
T I C K E T Y B O O   N A V Y
```

91

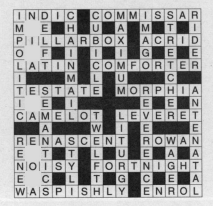

```
I N D I C   C O M M I S S A R
M   E   H   U   A   M   T   I
P I L L A R B O X   A C R I D
O   F   I   I   I   G   E   E
L A T I N   C O M F O R T E R
I       M   L   U       C
T E S T A T E   M O R P H I A
I   E   I       E   E   N
C A M E L O T   L E V E R E T
    A       W   I   E     E
R E N A S C E N T   R O W A N
E   T   T   L   U   E   A   A
N O I S Y   F O R T N I G H T
E   C   L   T   G   C   E   A
W A S P I S H L Y   E N R O L
```

92

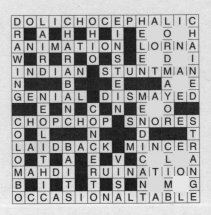

```
D O L I C H O C E P H A L I C
R   A   H   H   I   E   O   H
A N I M A T I O N   L O R N A
W   R   R   O   S   E   D   I
I N D I A N   S T U N T M A N
N   N   B   E       A   E
G E N I A L   D I S M A Y E D
    E   N   C   N   E   O
C H O P C H O P   S N O R E S
O   L   N       D       T
L A I D B A C K   M I N C E R
O   T   A   E   V   C   L   A
M A H D I   R U I N A T I O N
B   I   T   T   S   N   M   G
O C C A S I O N A L T A B L E
```

93

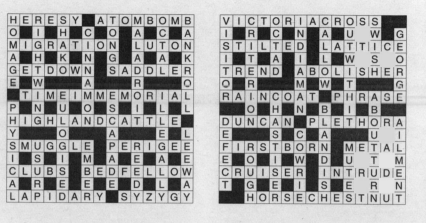

H	E	R	E	S	Y		A	T	O	M	B	O	M	B
O		I		H		C		O		A		C		A
M	I	G	R	A	T	I	O	N		L	U	T	O	N
A		H		K		N		G		A		A		K
G	E	T	D	O	W	N		S	A	D	D	L	E	R
E		W		A				A		R				O
	T	I	M	E	I	M	M	E	M	O	R	I	A	L
P		N		U		O		S		I		L		L
H	I	G	H	L	A	N	D	C	A	T	T	L	E	
Y		O		A				E				E		L
S	M	U	G	G	L	E		P	E	R	I	G	E	E
I		S		I		M		A		E		A		E
C	L	U	B	S		B	E	D	F	E	L	L	O	W
A		R		E		E		E		D		L		A
L	A	P	I	D	A	R	Y		S	Y	Z	Y	G	Y

94

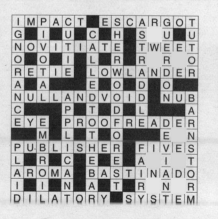

V	I	C	T	O	R	I	A	C	R	O	S	S		
I		R		C		N		A		U		W		G
S	T	I	L	T	E	D		L	A	T	T	I	C	E
I		T		A		I		L		W		S		O
T	R	E	N	D		A	B	O	L	I	S	H	E	R
O		R		M		W		T						G
R	A	I	N	C	O	A	T		P	H	R	A	S	E
		O		H		N		B		I		B		
D	U	N	C	A	N		P	L	E	T	H	O	R	A
E				S		C		A				U		I
F	I	R	S	T	B	O	R	N		M	E	T	A	L
E		O		I		W		D		U		T		M
C	R	U	I	S	E	R		I	N	T	R	U	D	E
T		G		E		I		S		E		R		N
	H	O	R	S	E	C	H	E	S	T	N	U	T	

95

H	E	A	D	W	O	R	D		L	I	Q	U	O	R
	D		R		S		R		I		U		P	
D	I	S	A	S	T	R	O	U	S		A	V	E	R
	T		Y		E		P		T		F		N	
		H	A	N	D	O	V	E	R	F	I	S	T	
	E		O		D		N		N				E	
D	Y	E	R			E	X	E	M	P	L	A	R	
	E		S		O		S		R		E		S	
S	W	E	E	T	P	E	A			P	R	O	P	
	I		T		I		Z		P		N			
S	T	O	C	K	I	N	T	R	A	D	E			
	N		A		C		C		G		R		B	
J	E	E	P		I	N	H	A	R	M	O	N	I	C
	S		R		A		E		E		N		L	
A	S	S	I	G	N		S	U	B	T	I	T	L	E

96

I	M	P	A	C	T		E	S	C	A	R	G	O	T
G		I		U		C		H		S		U		U
N	O	V	I	T	I	A	T	E		T	W	E	E	T
O		O		I		L		R		R		R		O
R	E	T	I	E		L	O	W	L	A	N	D	E	R
A		A		E		O		O		D		O		
N	U	L	L	A	N	D	V	O	I	D		N	U	B
C				P		T		D		L				A
E	Y	E		P	R	O	O	F	R	E	A	D	E	R
		M		L		T		O				E		N
P	U	B	L	I	S	H	E	R		F	I	V	E	S
L		R		C		E		E		A		I		T
A	R	O	M	A		B	A	S	T	I	N	A	D	O
I		I		N		A		T		R		N		R
D	I	L	A	T	O	R	Y		S	Y	S	T	E	M

SOLUTIONS

97

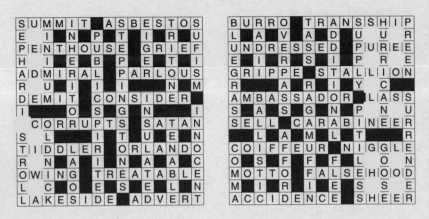

```
S U M M I T   A S B E S T O S
E   I N   P T   I   R   U
P E N T H O U S E   G R I E F
H   I   E B   P   E   T   I
A D M I R A L   P A R L O U S
R   U   I   I   I   N   M
D E M I T   C O N S I D E R
I     O   S   G   N     I
  C O R R U P T S   S A T A N
S   L   I   T   U   E   N
T I D D L E R   O R L A N D O
R   N   A   I   N   A A   C
O W I N G   T R E A T A B L E
L   C   O   E   S   E L   N
L A K E S I D E   A D V E R T
```

98

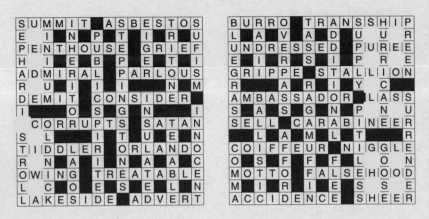

```
B U R R O   T R A N S S H I P
L   A V A   D   U   U   R
U N D R E S S E D   P U R E E
E   I   R   S   I   P   R E
G R I P P E   S T A L L I O N
R     A   R   I   Y   C
A M B A S S A D O R   L A S S
S   A   S   G   N   P   N U
S E L L   C A R A B I N E E R
L   A   M   L   T   R
C O I F F E U R   N I G G L E
O   S   F   F F   L   O N
M O T T O   F A L S E H O O D
M   I   R   I E   S   S E
A C C I D E N C E   S H E E R
```

99

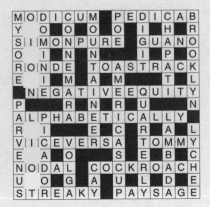

```
M O D I C U M   P E D I C A B
Y   O   O   O   I   H   R
S I M O N P U R E   G U A N O
O   I   N   N   I   P   O
R O N D E   T O A S T R A C K
E   I   M   A M   T   L
  N E G A T I V E E Q U I T Y
P     R   N   R   U     N
A L P H A B E T I C A L L Y
R   I   E   C   R   A   L
V I C E V E R S A   T O M M Y
E   A   O   S   E   B   C
N O D A L   C O C K R O A C H
U   O   G   A   U   L D   E
S T R E A K Y   P A Y S A G E
```

100

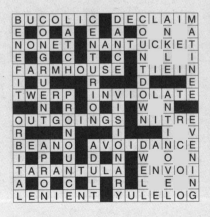

```
B U C O L I C   D E C L A I M
E   O   A   E A   O   N   A
N O N E T   N A N T U C K E T
E   G   C T   C   N   L   I
F A R M H O U S E   T I E I N
I   U     R   D   E
T W E R P   I N V I O L A T E
    N   R O   I   W   N
O U T G O I N G S   N I T R E
R   N   I   I   I   V
B E A N O   A V O I D A N C E
I   P   U D   N   W O   N
T A R A N T U L A   E N V O I
A   O   C L   R   L E   N
L E N I E N T   Y U L E L O G
```

101

102

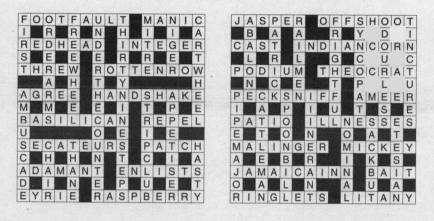

103

104

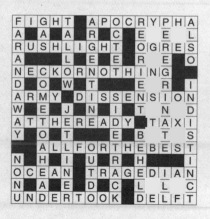

SOLUTIONS

105

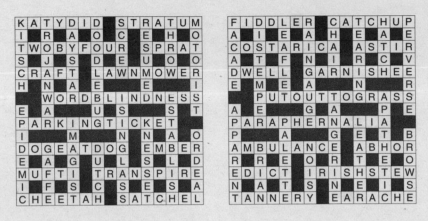

K	A	T	Y	D	I	D		S	T	R	A	T	U	M
I		R		A		O		C		E		H		O
T	W	O	B	Y	F	O	U	R		S	P	R	A	T
S		J		S		D		E		U		O		O
C	R	A	F	T			L	A	W	N	M	O	W	E	R
H		N		A		E			E			I
		W	O	R	D	B	L	I	N	D	N	E	S	S
E		A			U		S			S		S		T
P	A	R	K	I	N	G	T	I	C	K	E	T
I			M			N		N		A		O
D	O	G	E	A	T	D	O	G		E	M	B	E	R
E		A		G		U		L		S		L		D
M	U	F	T	I		T	R	A	N	S	P	I	R	E
I		F		S		C		S		E		S		A
C	H	E	E	T	A	H		S	A	T	C	H	E	L

106

F	I	D	D	L	E	R		C	A	T	C	H	U	P
A		I		E		A		H		E		A		E
C	O	S	T	A	R	I	C	A		A	S	T	I	R
A		T		F		N		I		R		C		V
D	W	E	L	L		G	A	R	N	I	S	H	E	E
E		M		E		A			N			R
		P	U	T	O	U	T	T	O	G	R	A	S	S
A		E			G		A			P		E
P	A	R	A	P	H	E	R	N	A	L	I	A
P			A			G		E		T		B
A	M	B	U	L	A	N	C	E		A	B	H	O	R
R		R		E		O		R		T		E		O
E	D	I	C	T		I	R	I	S	H	S	T	E	W
N		A		S		N		N		E		I		S
T	A	N	N	E	R	Y		E	A	R	A	C	H	E

107

C	R	O	S	S	C	U	T		H	U	B	B	U	B
	H		L		O		O		O		R		A
Q	U	E	E	N	S		T	U	R	N	D	O	W	N
	B		E		S		H		S		T		D
C	A	M	P	S	I	T	E		E	S	C	H	E	W
	R		W		E		M		B		E		I
A	B	E	A	M		A	A	R	O	N	S	R	O	D
R		L		F		N		X		U		T
T	A	L	K	R	O	U	N	D		A	B	A	S	H
E		O		O		E		P		J		E
M	O	Z	A	R	T		R	E	L	I	E	V	E	D
I		E		P		B		A		C		D
S	A	N	T	I	A	G	O		N	U	T	K	I	N
I		G		T		R		C		E		L
A	W	E	I	G	H		N	A	K	E	D	E	Y	E

108

P	A	T	H	E	T	I	C		R	E	S	I	G	N
	I		A		H		R		E		C		O
B	R	O	W	N	E	D	O	F	F		R	U	F	F
	E		K		B		S		I		U		O
			S	T	A	R	S	A	N	D	B	A	R	S
	F		M		N		W		E		B
T	O	G	O			O	N	R	E	C	O	R	D
	R		O		N		R		Y		A		O
R	E	A	R	W	A	R	D			R	A	K	E
	R		M		P		I		E		E
H	U	B	B	L	E	B	U	B	B	L	E
	N		L		D		Z		E		R		A
A	N	T	I		R	A	Z	O	R	B	I	L	L	S
	E		M		O		L		I		S		T
W	R	A	P	U	P		E	X	A	C	T	I	O	N

109

110

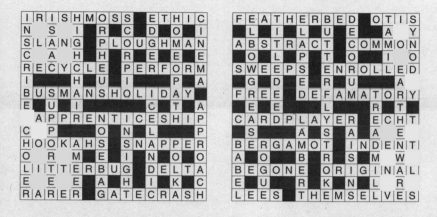

111

112

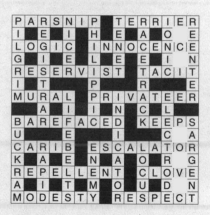

SOLUTIONS

113

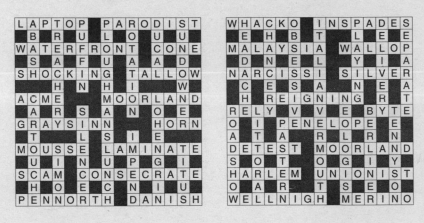

```
L A P T O P   P A R O D I S T
  B   R   U   L   O   U   U
W A T E R F R O N T   C O N E
  S   A   F   U   A   A   D
S H O C K I N G   T A L L O W
  H   N   H   I       W
A C M E     M O O R L A N D
  A   R   S   A   N   O   E
G R A Y S I N N     H O R N
  T   L   S   I   E
M O U S S E   L A M I N A T E
  U   I   N   U   P   G   I
S C A M   C O N S E C R A T E
  H   O   E   C   N   I   U
P E N N O R T H   D A N I S H
```

114

```
W H A C K O   I N S P A D E S
  E   H   B   T   L   E   E
M A L A Y S I A   W A L L O P
  D   N   E   L   Y   I   A
N A R C I S S I   S I L V E R
  C   E   S   A   N   E   A
  H   R E I G N I N G   R   T
R E L Y   V   V   E   B Y T E
O   I   P E N E L O P E   E
A   T   A   R   L   R   N
D E T E S T   M O O R L A N D
S   O   T   O   G   I   Y
H A R L E M   U N I O N I S T
O   A   R   T   S   E   O
W E L L N I G H   M E R I N O
```

115

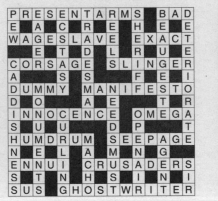

```
P R E S E N T A R M S   B A D
E   A   C   R   E   H   E   E
W A G E S L A V E   E X A C T
  E   T   D   L   R   U   E
C O R S A G E   S L I N G E R
A   S   S   F   E   I
D U M M Y   M A N I F E S T O
D   O   A   E   T   R
I N N O C E N C E   O M E G A
S   U   U   D   P   T
H U M D R U M   S E E P A G E
N   E   L   A   M   N   G
E N N U I   C R U S A D E R S
S   T   N   H   S   I   N   I
S U S   G H O S T W R I T E R
```

116

```
T O N S U R E   T I M P A N I
O   A   P   P   R   A   N   N
S E R V E T I M E   S T A I D
S   W   N   L   B   O   G   E
    H Y D R O E L E C T R I C
A   A   G   E   H   A   I
C A L C U L U S   L I T M U S
C   R   E   I   S   I   O
E X C I T E   F L A M I N G O
S   O   I   U   L   I   N
S E M I C O N D U C T O R
I   P   A   U   S   U   V   F
B R I E R   S H O R T G A M E
L   L   I   E   R   O   N   T
E M E R A L D   Y A R D A G E
```

117

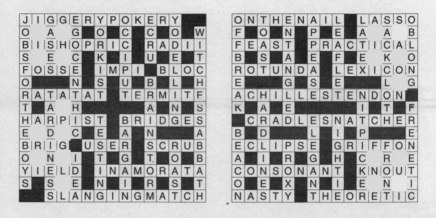

118

119

120

SOLUTIONS

121

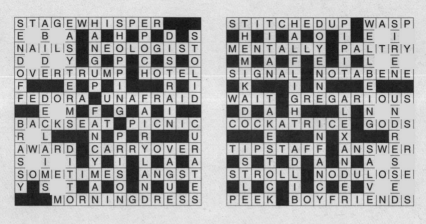

S T A G E W H I S P E R
E B A A H P D S
N A I L S N E O L O G I S T
D D Y G P C S O
O V E R T R U M P H O T E L
F E P I R I
F E D O R A U N A F R A I D
E M F G A I
B A C K S E A T P I C N I C
R L N P R U
A W A R D C A R R Y O V E R
S I I Y I L A A
S O M E T I M E S A N G S T
Y S T A O N U E
M O R N I N G D R E S S

122

S T I T C H E D U P W A S P
H I A O I E I
M E N T A L L Y P A L T R Y
M A F E I L E
S I G N A L N O T A B E N E
K I N E
W A I T G R E G A R I O U S
D A H L N N
C O C K A T R I C E G O D S
E N X R
T I P S T A F F A N S W E R
S T D A N A S
S T R O L L N O D U L O S E
L C I C E V E
P E E K B O Y F R I E N D S

123

D E C I S I O N E S C H E W
E E W R K H O A
C A S T I N G D I R E C T O R
A T T A N L E L
D O L P H I N G A L I L E O
E A I L E C
O V E N W A R E Y A P O K
E I U A A S
S P E C S T A R T A R U S
T P O B L E
R E B O U N D B L U E J A Y
A O R A O S O E
N O N P R O F E S S I O N A L
G G E E U V E I
E P O N Y M U N V E R S E D

124

S E L F C R I T I C I S M
U I A N N N O
A P E S B A S S O F E L L
E L R U F I O
A R T E R I A L F I E S T A
N O I L O
G A N G P L A N K S D O V E
T R E U E C
T U N A T I R I N G R O O M
R N I S C
H A N D L E C A T W A L K S
L S L O R D T
D I A L I N T R O M O A T
S A T T K I I
T E M P E R A M E N T A L

SOLUTIONS

125

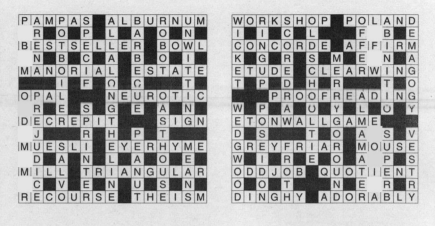

```
P A M P A S   A L B U R N U M
R   O   P   L   A   O   N
B E S T S E L L E R   B O W L
N   B   C   A   B   O   I
M A N O R I A L   E S T A T E
  I   F   O   C       T
O P A L   N E U R O T I C
R   E   S   G   E   A   N
D E C R E P I T   S I G N
  J   R   H   P   T
M U E S L I   E Y E R H Y M E
  D   A   N   L   A   O   E
M I L L   T R I A N G U L A R
  C   V   E   N   U   S   N
R E C O U R S E   T H E I S M
```

126

```
W O R K S H O P   P O L A N D
I   I   C   L   F   B   E
C O N C O R D E   A F F I R M
K   G   R   S   M   E   N A
E T U D E   C L E A R W I N G
T   P   D   H   R   T   O
    P R O O F R E A D I N G
W   P   A   U   Y   L   U Y
E T O N W A L L G A M E
D   S   T   O   A   S   V
G R E Y F R I A R   M O U S E
W   I   R   E   O   A   P S
O D D J O B   Q U O T I E N T
O   O   T   N   E   R   R
D I N G H Y   A D O R A B L Y
```

127

```
L O V A G E   L O N G S T O P
V   N   S   I   R   A   I
J E T T I S O N   T I F F I N
R   I   E   E   M   F   P
F L A M I N G O   H A I R D O
O   O   T   N   C   A   I
O   N O I S E T T E   I   N
O K A Y   A   S   H   S L I T
U   P   C L A P T R A P   M
T   P   H   O   E   E   M
R O L L E R   C A S H C R O P
I   Y   S   K   H   I   R
D A I N T Y   E N O R M I T Y
E   N   E   T   L   E   A
R I G O R O U S   D A N G L E
```

128

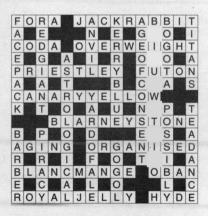

```
F O R A   J A C K R A B B I T
A   E       N   E   G O   I
C O D A   O V E R W E I G H T
E   G   A   I   R   O O   A
P R I E S T L E Y   F U T O N
A   A   T   B   C   A   S
C A N A R Y Y E L L O W
K   T   O   A   U   N P   T
    B L A R N E Y S T O N E
B   P   O   D   E   S   A
A G I N G   O R G A N I S E D
R   R   I   F   O   T   I A
B L A N C M A N G E   O B A N
E   C   A   L   O   L   C
R O Y A L J E L L Y   H Y D E
```

SOLUTIONS

129

130

131

132

133

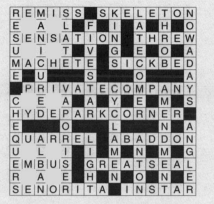

```
R E M I S S ▪ S K E L E T O N
E   A   L   F   I   A   H   O
S E N S A T I O N ▪ T H R E W
U   I   T   V   G   E   O   A
M A C H E T E ▪ S I C K B E D
E   U       S   O   A   A
▪ P R I V A T E C O M P A N Y
C   E   A   A   Y   E   M   S
H Y D E P A R K C O R N E R ▪
E       O       L       N   A
Q U A R R E L ▪ A B A D D O N
U   L   I   I   M   N   M   G
E M B U S ▪ G R E A T S E A L
R   A   E   H   N   O   N   E
S E N O R I T A ▪ I N S T A R
```

134

```
T R O C H E E ▪ I N C O M E R
E   T   I   N   N   O   E   E
M O T I V A T E D ▪ M E A N S
P   O   E   R   A   M   N   U
▪ M A S T E R B U I L D E R ▪
S   A   A   A   T   E   G
H A N D O U T S ▪ S T A R V E
O   V   Y   C   E       N
V A I N E R ▪ D O M E S T I C
E   N   R   G   N   I   E
L E V E L C R O S S I N G ▪
L   O   A   O   U   V   H   I
I L I A D ▪ C O M F O R T E D
N   C   E   E   E   R   E   L
G L E A N E R ▪ D O Y E N N E
```

135

```
R I P R O A R I N G ▪ A B E T
O   E   V   U   E       E   E
V I L L E I N A G E ▪ C L A N
E   T   R   I   L   F   L   D
▪ R E I N V I G O R A T E ▪
S   A   S   G   R   D   R
E M P A T H I S E ▪ M A O R I
M   P   I   M   N   A   N   S
I L E U M ▪ P E T U L A N C E
Q   N   A   O   D   A   D
U N D E T E R M I N E D ▪
A   I   E   T   S   H   H   O
V I C E ▪ P A S T R Y C O O K
E   E   N   L   D   W   A
R U S K ▪ F T H E R F A I L Y
```

136

```
▪ M U S I C A L C H A I R S ▪
I   U   L   I   I   N   A
A D A M ▪ O U T E R ▪ S U I T
D   A   S   E   A   O   L
A L L C L E A R ▪ M A L A W I
E       C   A       V   I
C O D S W A L L O P ▪ E A T S
F   C   L   E   N   H
I T C H ▪ L I E I N S T A T E
H   O   P   S   H
M E M O I R ▪ H E I G H T E N
R   L   A   E   O   I   T
F O R M ▪ I B S E N ▪ N E I L
A   E   S   U   E   D   D
D I N N E R S E R V I C E ▪
```

SOLUTIONS

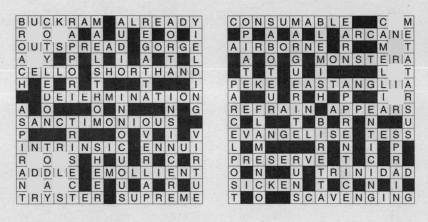

137

BUCKRAM ALREADY / ROA AU EO I / OUTSPREAD GORGE / AY P L I A T L / CELLO SHORTHAND / H ERT T I / DETERMINATION / A O O N N G / SANCTIMONIOUS / P R OV I V / INTRINSIC ENNUI / R OS H UR C R / ADDLE EMOLLIENT / N AC E UA R U / TRYSTER SUPREME

138

CONSUMABLE C M / P AA L ARCANE E / AIRBORNE R M T / A OG MONSTERA / T TU I LT / PEKE EASTANGLIA / A UR H P IR / REFRAIN APPEARS / C L T BR N U / EVANGELISE TESS / L M R N I P / PRESERVE T C R / O N U TRINIDAD / SICKEN T C N I / T O SCAVENGING

139

BENCHMARK FLUNG / A OE R EL NO / RESTART GLOTTAL / OER I R RD / NIGHT CASTASIDE / A AU I EN / MAY CALLTOORDER / E CH AT V O / LOOSESTRIFE SAD / O N EN R E / DOGEATDOG BESOM / R OG R OT I / ABIGAIL OVATION / MN P EOR NC / ANGLE IMMEDIATE

140

BECKYSHARP CHEF / R AE OE E R / IRRELEVANT EASE / G DL EA CR I / WORLDSHAKING / H FW C BN H / OBEISANCE INGOT / SAT IN NAA / PETER GATHERING / I HE H TD E / THELASTTRUMP / ARK LA AUD / BABE MISTAKENLY / L E FT EIE / EDDY DEHYDRATOR

SOLUTIONS

141

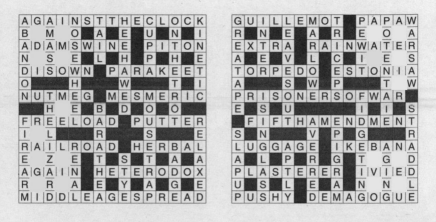

```
A G A I N S T T H E C L O C K
B M O A E U N I
A D A M S W I N E P I T O N
N S E L H P H E
D I S O W N P A R A K E E T
O H W T I
N U T M E G M E S M E R I C
H E B D O O
F R E E L O A D P U T T E R
I L R S E
R A I L R O A D H E R B A L
E Z E T S T A A
A G A I N H E T E R O D O X
R R A E Y A G E
M I D D L E A G E S P R E A D
```

142

```
G U I L L E M O T P A P A W
R N E A R E O A
E X T R A R A I N W A T E R
A E V L C I E S
T O R P E D O E S T O N I A
A A S W P T W
P R I S O N E R S O F W A R
E S U I I S
F I F T H A M E N D M E N T
S N V P G R
L U G G A G E I K E B A N A
A L P R G T G D
P L A S T E R E R I V I E D
U S L E A N N L
P U S H Y D E M A G O G U E
```

143

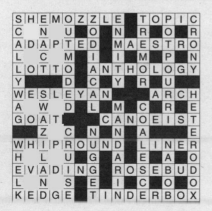

```
S H E M O Z Z L E T O P I C
C N U O N R O R
A D A P T E D M A E S T R O
L C M I I M P N
L O T T O A N T H O L O G Y
Y D C Y R U
W E S L E Y A N A R C H
A W D L M C R E
G O A T C A N O E I S T
Z C N N A E
W H I P R O U N D L I N E R
H L U G A E A O
E V A D I N G R O S E B U D
L N S E I C O O
K E D G E T I N D E R B O X
```

144

```
C H A F F I N C H B O S O M
O N A U O L I O
M A G I C R E L I E F M A P
M R E E D S U P
O D Y S S E Y A B S O L V E
N U E L A T
E S C A P E V E L O C I T Y
R O T O O A
O U T O F T H I S W O R L D
C R O N R A
H I G H W A Y S A I L A R M
I E O S T T N S
P E T R U C H I O T I K K A
P T N O C E L L
Y I E L D P E K I N G E S E
```

SOLUTIONS

145

```
  W H I P P I N G P O S T
F   I   R   A   I   O   U
I G N E O U S   S O F A B E D
S   D   N   O   E   A   S   O
H U S B A N D   I S C H I U M
A   O   G   O   E   D   I
N O R S E   B R O A D B E A N
D       L   N           O
C O M P O N E N T   C L E F T
H   A   S   H   H   T   H
I S T H M U S   E M A N A T E
P   I   O   W   N   P   G   O
S I L E S I A   A M A T E U R
    D   I   M   I   T   R   Y
  M A R S E I L L A I S E
```

146

```
Y O R K S H I R E D A L E S
O   E   T   N   F   C   V   K
U N H E A R D O F   C H I D E
R   O   L   I   E   E   D   E
E Q U A L   G O T O S L E E P
T   S   E   E   E   S   N   O
E L E P H A N T   B I T T E N
L   E   T   O   O       E
L U S T R A   P R I N C E S S
I   C   C   C   I       P   C
N U R T U R I N G   W E I G H
G   A   L   R   I   A   T   I
M A T T E   C O N S T R A I N
E   C   A   L   A   E   P   U
  C H A N C E L L O R S H I P
```

147

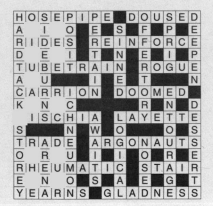

```
H O S E P I P E   D O U S E D
A   I   O   E   S   F   P   E
R I D E S   R E I N F O R C E
D   E   I   T   N   E   I   P
T U B E T R A I N   R O G U E
A   U   I   E   T       N
C A R R I O N   D O O M E D
K   N   C       R   N   D
  I S C H I A   L A Y E T T E
S   N   W   O   O       O   S
T R A D E   A R G O N A U T S
O   R   U   I   I   O   R   E
R H E U M A T I C   S T A I R
E   N   O   S   A   E   G   T
Y E A R N S   G L A D N E S S
```

148

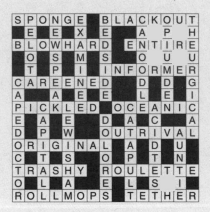

```
S P O N G E   B L A C K O U T
  E   E   X   E   A   P   H
B L O W H A R D   E N T I R E
  O   S   M   S   O   U   U
  T   P   I   I N F O R M E R
C A R E E N E D   D   D   G
A   A   E   E   L   E   I
P I C K L E D   O C E A N I C
E   A   E   D   A   C   A
D   P   W   O U T R I V A L
O R I G I N A L   A   D   U
C   T   S   O   P   T   N
T R A S H Y   R O U L E T T E
O   L   A   E   L   S   I
R O L L M O P S   T E T H E R
```

149

```
A R C H A I C   C O C K P I T
C H   V   A   O   R   A   R
C H A R A C T E R   U N D U E
E   P   L   E   S   L   A
D R A M A   R E L A T I O N S
E   T   N   P   I     C   U
  C I R C U I T B R E A K E R
S     H   L   E   X     Y
P R O P E L L E R S H A F T
A   F     A   T   A   I   C
C A F E T E R I A   U T T E R
E   H   O     R   S   N   I
B R A W N   P O I N T L E S S
A   N   I   A   A   E   S   I
R A D I C A L   N U D I S T S
```

150

```
S A I N T P A U L   A R K L E
K   M   E   P   O   B   E   L
I M P I N G E   V A L E R I E
P   L   D   R   I   O   B   G
J O Y C E   T E N U O U S L Y
A     R   U   G   M   T
C O B B L E R S     F O L D
K   O   Y   E   F   S   N   A
S T A G     D O M I N E E R
  T   H   T   L   C     T
B E T R O T H A L   K R O N A
E   R   O   O   O   N   R   G
A N A G R A M   W O O D M A N
C   I   A   A   O   T   E   A
H E N R Y   S A N H E D R I N
```

151

```
G R I Z Z L E D   A G R E E D
O   G   L   X   B   R   L   Y
L E N T O   P R I V A T I O N
D   O   T   L   C   N   O   A
D I R T Y W O R K   D A T U M
U   A   I   E   T   O
S U N S P O T   R I O T E D
T   C   A     U   S   C
  D E N I E R   A G R I P P A
S     L   U   D   E   R
A P P A L   B R A S S E R I E
U   R   A   B   P   U   A   L
C R O W S F E E T   M I N K E
E   N   S   R   O   A   T   S
R A G G E D   P R E C I O U S
```

152

```
F I G H T B A C K   R I G I D
A   E   O   S   E   E   N   I
C E N T U R Y   W E A P O N S
E   T   C   O   L   S   E
T H I G H   U L T I M A T U M
  A   D   L   H   I   B
S O N   O B I T E R D I C T A
M   W   K   R   E     R
A R R A N G E M E N T   A R K
R   A   I   Y   R   N
T I M B U C T O O   I L I U M
A   P   N   U   M   M   A
L E A N I N G   A M E N I T Y
E   N   T   A   R   N   S   O
C A T T Y   S P E C T A T O R
```

SOLUTIONS

153

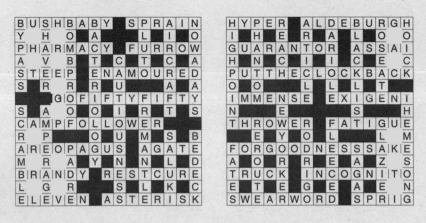

154

155

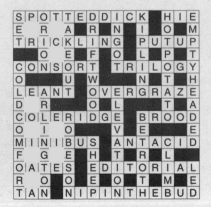

156

157

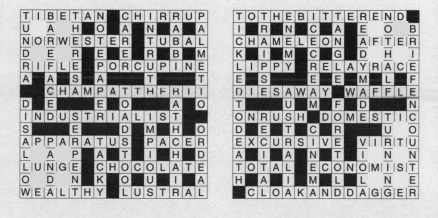

```
T I B E T A N   C H I R R U P
U A H O   A   N A A   A
N O R W E S T E R   T U B A L
D E R   E   E   R B   M
R I F L E   P O R C U P I N E
A A S A   T       T
  C H A M P A T T H E B I T
D E   E O       A   O
I N D U S T R I A L I S T
S   E     D   M H     O
A P P A R A T U S   P A C E R
L A P A   T   I H   D
L U N G E   C H O C O L A T E
O D N   K   O U   I A
W E A L T H Y   L U S T R A L
```

158

```
T O T H E B I T T E R E N D
I   R N C A   E O   B
C H A M E L E O N   A F T E R
K   I M C G   D H   I
L I P P Y   R E L A Y R A C E
E   S   E E M   L F
D I E S A W A Y   W A F F L E
T   U M F D       N
O N R U S H   D O M E S T I C
D E T C R   U   O
E X C U R S I V E   V I R T U
A I A N T   I N N
T O T A L   E C O N O M I S T
H A I M L   L N E
  C L O A K A N D D A G G E R
```

159

```
E X T R A O R D I N A R Y
X I N E M   S I A
A M M O N I A   P A T T E R N
M E E P A R   L O
P H L O X   P H I L A N D E R
L A E R K   A A
E S P E C I A L   S H R I N K
S A R C A N
B L E A R Y   M A G N E T I C
I E B T   E H
S U B S T R A T A   D I R G E
E L A R C E L D
C R I C K E T   O F F L O A D
T S E O M O C A
  S T R I K E B R E A K E R
```

160

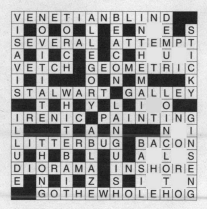

```
V E N E T I A N B L I N D
I O O L   E N E   S
S E V E R A L   A T T E M P T
A I C E C H U I
V E T C H   G E O M E T R I C
I I O N M K
S T A L W A R T   G A L L E Y
T H Y L I O
I R E N I C   P A I N T I N G
L T A N N I
L I T T E R B U G   B A C O N
U H B L U A L S
D I O R A M A   I N S H O R E
E N I Z S I T N
  G O T H E W H O L E H O G
```

TIMESONLINE

¹A	R	²C	H	³I	V	⁴E	S		5		⁶S
	■		■		■		■	⁷B	U	N	T
⁸P	R	I	N	T	A	B	L	E			O
	■		■		■		■		⁹I	N	K
¹⁰C	L	U	B		■	¹¹C	R	A	S	E	E

Finished already?
The crosswords never stop at
The Times Crossword Club

Premium Club features:

- Printable and interactive versions of cryptic, concise and jumbo crosswords from *The Times* and *The Sunday Times*
- Additional puzzles, including *The Listener*, Mephisto and *Times Literary Supplement*
- The chance to win £100 in our exclusive – and extra difficult – monthly prize crossword
- Full archive of puzzles dating back to 2000, plus a selection of vintage puzzles from The Times archive
- A monthly e-mail bulletin with the latest club news and views
- Save partially completed crosswords – you can bookmark and return to complete your puzzles at a later date
- Enter *Times* and *Sunday Times* crossword competitions by e-mail with our easy-to-submit interactive format
- Buy a club membership for friends and family, including a personalised e-mail. The ideal gift for your favourite cruciverbalist

Try our free demonstration at:
www.timesonline.co.uk/crossword

TIMES ONLINE
Home
News
Britain
World
Business
Your Money
Sport
Sports Book
Comment
Travel
Entertainment
Law
Crossword
Driving
Property
Health
Jobs
Food and drink
Books
Student
Site Map